0

A WEEK WITH

GANDHI

also by LOUIS FISCHER

MEN AND POLITICS

DAWN OF VICTORY

A WEEK WITH
GANDHI

LOUIS FISCHER

ILLUSTRATED

NEW YORK · DUELL, SLOAN AND PEARCE

Author's Note

This little volume is published through no fault of mine. I kept a careful diary during the week I spent with Gandhi. Lest those notes be lost or destroyed I wrote them out after I returned to America. A number of friends saw the manuscript and urged me to let it be published in full. I argued that it would be a very incomplete account of my visit to India. I had had many other talks in India which were important but off the record, I said. A book on Gandhi alone would not be a comprehensive book on India. "That's all right," my friends replied, "say so in a foreword." I am saying so now.

My talks with Gandhi were a rich, stimulating experience. Lord Linlithgow, the Viceroy at New Delhi, said to me, "Gandhi is the biggest thing in India." That is correct. Gandhi is a unique phenomenon. Contact with his personality and mind is exciting. I made an almost stenographic record of everything he said to me. I reproduce it in the following pages. My own comments on Gandhi will be found in a short last chapter.

A WEEK WITH

GANDHI

June 3, 1942

AFTER twenty-seven hours in the hot, dusty express train from New Delhi, I arrived in Wardha, a small town in Central India, at 8:30 P. M. Ten days earlier I had asked Jawaharlal Nehru to arrange an interview with Gandhi for me. In a few days Nehru wrote from Wardha saying that Gandhi would see me. He advised me to get into touch with Mahadev Desai, Gandhi's secretary, to fix the time. I informed Desai that any time would do and he wired back: "Welcome—Mahadev Desai."

As I stepped out of the train at Wardha, a young man in white approached me and asked whether I was Fischer; when I said yes, he told me he had been delegated by Gandhi to meet me. A tonga was waiting. A tonga is a one-horse, two-wheeled carriage in which the passengers sit behind the driver with their backs to the horse. We drove through the darkness to the outskirts of town and got out at a house which an Indian millionaire nationalist had bequeathed to the Congress Party for use as a hostel. I slept on a big second-story porch open to the sky. All night an orange-white-green Congress flag fluttered with a kind of Morse-code noise.

I was up early and took a tonga with Gandhi's dentist for Sevagram, the village which is Gandhi's home when he is not in jail. The dentist said that England had been "an understanding master." I tried to make him talk about Gandhi. He insisted on talking politics.

The tonga stopped. I jumped out and there stood a tall, brown-and-white figure—Gandhi. I walked towards him with long, quick steps. He held his hand on the shoulders of two women who walked on either side of him. His thin brown legs were bare up to his loincloth. Leather sandals on his feet; a cape of cheesecloth around his shoulders; a folded white kerchief on his head. He said, "Mr. Fischer," with an English accent, and we shook hands. He greeted the dentist, turned about, and I followed him to a flat, thick board resting on two metal trestles. He sat down, put his hand on the board, and said, "Sit down." He said, "Jawaharlal has told me about your book and the type of person you are, and we are glad to have you here. How long will you stay?" I told him I could stay a few days.

"Oh," he exclaimed, "then we will be able to talk much."

A young man walked over to him, bowed low to his feet, and swayed up and down. "Bas, bas," Gandhi muttered. I imagined it meant "Enough," and later found that my guess was right. Soon two other young men did the same thing, and again Gandhi shooed them off.

I asked him why he had chosen this village to live in. He said so-and-so, and he mentioned a name which I didn't get, had chosen it for him. I made no comment, but he noticed that I didn't catch the Indian name, and so he said Mira Ben was Miss Slade, an Englishwoman who had long been associated with him. He explained that it was her idea that he should live in a village in the center of India, and he had asked her to find the place. He did not wish to live inside the village because it was too unhygienic and noisy. "It is better here, on the outskirts." The dentist started talking about false teeth, and Gandhi explained to him that the bite in the sets he wore was imperfect. A woman brought out a brass bowl filled with water and three sets of artificial teeth, and I decided to go. Gandhi said, "You will walk with me in the evening and morning, and we will have other opportunities to talk." I bowed and went away.

I was given the freedom of Sevagram's guest house—a one-room mud hut with earthen floor and bamboo roof. There are several beds in the room. Leading from the room is a tiny kitchen and also a water room with a stone floor on which stood a large number of tin and brass buckets and two tin washtubs, which "Bai"—the aged maid— kept filling with water carried in jars on her head from the village well. Gandhi had told me that I would be in the care of Kurshed Ben, or Sister Kurshed. Miss Kurshed Naoroji is a Parsi, aged about forty. She wore a coarse yellow home-spun sari. She had studied singing in France and Italy for six years, but had dropped her musical career fifteen years ago and has since been a con-stant disciple of Gandhi. Her family are million-aires. Her grandfather, who died during the first World War at the age of ninety-five, was the first Indian member of the British House of Commons. Saklatvala, another Parsi—and a Communist, was the third and last Indian member of the British Parliament.

Kurshed Ben is intelligent and quick. I argue with her that there has been an overemphasis here on Indian nationalism. An independent India, I contend, might become Fascist, and then it would have less freedom than under the British. She rejects this reasoning. She wants the British out first, and then the Indians will solve their own problems. "We want to be alone," Kurshed said. "It is like a housewife who has had guests staying with her for too long, and she is impatient to see them leave, and can think of nothing else but the pleasure of the moment when she sees them going out through the front door."

Kurshed took me visiting to several members of the Gandhi "ashram," or community. They are all Congress field-workers or Gandhi's secretaries, or just people who arrive and stay for a while to sit at the naked feet of the master. They come from various parts of India, and sometimes speak different Indian languages, so that they must communicate with one another in English. The children are very beautiful. I stopped in at Mahadev Desai's hut. I found him, bald and paunchy, dressed only in a loincloth, sitting on a floor mat spinning on a primitive "charka." His wife was in the next room, clothed in a much-twisted sari, doing likewise. Desai spins five hundred yards a day. The charka is a very simple machine which any peasant could make or buy cheaply. Desai said he travels a good deal and spins on trains. But he had never noticed anybody else doing it. Thanks to Gandhi's propaganda and personal example, hundreds of thousands of Indian peasants had taken up home spinning in order to develop village industry and pro-

vide clothes for the almost-naked millions. "But
the habit has not spread very far," Desai admitted,
"and spinning is no factor in India's national
economy."

At eleven A. M., when I was starved, Kurshed
took me over to Gandhi's house, which is about a
hundred yards from the guest house. It is a one-
story affair with walls of matting and a roof of
poor red tiles. I left my bedroom slippers on the
outside cement step and walked in and remained
in the tiny anteroom from which I could see the
one chief room of the house. Gandhi was lying on
a white pallet on the earthen floor, and one of his
disciples sat on the ground near this bed and
pulled a rope which moved a board, with a black
cloth hanging from it, suspended from the ceiling.
This is supposed to take the place of an electric
fan. There is no electricity in the village. Gandhi
got up and said to me, "Now put on your shoes
and hat. Those are the two indispensable things
here. Don't get a sunstroke." A woman brought
him a folded, moistened cheesecloth for his head.
Then, putting one hand on Kurshed, who walked
one step in front of him, he said to me in friendly
fashion, "Come along." We passed two houses and
came to a common dining hall built of matting. I
left my shoes outside, as Gandhi did, gave my sun
helmet to Kurshed, who found a place for it on a
peg on the wall, and took a seat on the ground

which Gandhi indicated, two removed from him.
Between us was the asthmatic Narendra Dev, a
leader of the Indian Socialist Party which is affili-
ated with Congress. I sat down on a strip of matting about a foot wide. Gandhi sat on a pillow. To
his left was his toothless wife, Kasturba. She is
seventy. He is seventy-three.

The dining hall has two long walls connected
by a third back wall. Where one enters, it is open
to the elements. Near the entrance is a table covered with jars and trays of food. The women sit
apart. I watched some bright-eyed, brown-faced
children, some of them three, five or eight years
old, the children of the members of the ashram.
Soon every person had a brass tray in front of him,
and several waiters were moving noiselessly on
bare feet, depositing food on the trays. Several pots
and pans were placed before Gandhi. He opened
them and started dishing out food to his neighbors.
I had been given a metal tumbler full of water.
Gandhi handed me a bronze bowl filled with a
vegetable mush in which I thought I discerned
chopped spinach leaves and pieces of squash. Then
he uncovered a metal container and gave me one
hard, paper-thin wheatcake. A woman poured
some salt into my tray and handed me a bowl of
hot milk. Soon she came back with two boiled
potatoes in their jackets and some soft, flat wheatcakes baked brown. Gandhi turned to me and said,

with a smile, "I am serving you, but you must not eat until the prayer." I told him I had noticed that the children were not touching their food and so I knew I mustn't. The thirty-odd people in the room, all dressed in white and squatting on the brown floor, were receiving their food and not eating it. Diners passed food to one another with their hands. A gong sounded, and a tall, healthy-looking man in white shorts stopped waiting on the trays and closed his eyes, leaving only a white slit open—it made him look blind—and started a high-pitched chant in which all the others, including Gandhi, joined. The prayer ended with "shaanti, shaanti, shaanti," which, Dev told me, means "peace."

I had been given a teaspoon for the vegetable mess, but most people fished it out with their round wheatcakes folded in four. A woman waitress poured some liquid butter on my wheatcakes. With a liberal use of salt, the food was not too untasty. I got some sugar to take away the taste of the boiled cow-milk (Gandhi has given up goat-milk and now encourages the consumption of cow-milk throughout India in the hope that more attention will be paid to the breeding of healthy cattle).

Gandhi ate continuously, only stopping to serve food to his wife, Kurshed, Dev, and me. His hands are big and his fingers are big and well-formed.

His knees are pronounced bulges and his bones are wide and strong. His skin is smooth and clean. His hands do not shake as he digs into the pots. His wife fanned him frequently with a straw fan. She looks the symbol of silent self-effacement.

Once Gandhi interrupted to say, "You have lived in Russia for fourteen years. What is your opinion of Stalin?"

I felt very hot, and my hands were sticky, and so I replied briefly, "Very able and very ruthless."

"As ruthless as Hitler?" Gandhi asked.

"At least," I replied.

After a pause, Gandhi turned to me again and said, "Have you seen the Viceroy?"

"Yes," I said, but Gandhi dropped the subject.

I was discovering my ankles. Too much of my weight was resting on them. The Indians know how to distribute their bodily weight, but I hadn't learned. I stood one leg on its foot, and felt a bit more comfortable. Gandhi said to me, "I see you have come to a standstill."

"No," I replied, "I find the food surprisingly good."

"You can have all the water you want," he said. "We take good care that it is boiled. And now you must eat your mango."

I said I had been observing others eat it, and would now, for the first time in my life, try one. Kurshed suggested that I would need a bath when

I was through. I started peeling the mango. Gandhi and others laughed. Gandhi explained that they usually turned it in their hands and squeezed it to make it soft, and then sucked out the contents, but I was right to peel it to see whether it was good. He said, "You will earn a medal of courage for being ready to eat as we do." I had finished the meal and Kurshed indicated with her head that I could go before Gandhi got up. I bowed to him, got my hat and shoes, and left. Kurshed said Gandhi would see me at three.

Indians usually do not shake hands. When they meet or part, they put their two palms together at the level of their mouths, smile sweetly, and sway. It makes them look very kindly and innocent. When I bowed to Gandhi, he gave me the touch-palm goodbye.

I went home, slept from twelve to one, and got up covered with perspiration. I took my third bath of the day in the water room; I simply stood and poured water over me from a small bronze vessel.

At a few minutes to three, I walked across the hundred yards of hot gravel and sand which separated my house from Gandhi's. The heat made the whole inside of my head feel dry. The temperature was a hundred and ten. When I entered Gandhi's room, six men in white were sitting on the floor of his room. A woman in a black sari was pulling the rope of the fan. There was only one decoration in the room, a glass-covered, black-and-white print of Jesus Christ, on which were printed the words, "He is our peace." Gandhi sat on the pallet which is his bed. There was a board behind his back and a pillow between the board and his back. He was wearing gold-rimmed glasses, and writing a letter with a fountain pen. His legs were crossed scissors-fashion. He held a small board on one knee, and on the board was the pad on which he wrote. Three other fountain pens stood in holes in a hand-made wooden stand. Left of his bed were some books piled neatly on the floor. He said to me, "Come sit down in the coolest place here beside the woman working the fan." I sat down in a corner and leaned my back against the matting. Gandhi said, "If you do not mind, these people will remain here. They will not speak. If you object, they can go." Dev was there and Desai, and several other members of the ashram, including Kurshed. I did not very much like the idea of an interview in company, but I said, "No," and got settled.

"Now I am fully at your disposal," Gandhi announced.

I said, "I feel that the Cripps mission was a turning point in Indian history. The country is probably now beginning to grasp the significance of Cripps's failure, and from that understanding big things might flow. I therefore wish to know why, in your opinion, Cripps failed."

"When Cripps arrived," Gandhi began, "he sent me a telegram asking me to come see him in New Delhi. I did not wish to go, but I went because I thought it would do some good. I had heard rumors about the contents of the British government's offer he brought to India, but I had not seen the offer. He gave it to me, and after a brief study, I said to him, 'Why did you come if this is what you have to offer? If this is your entire proposal to India, I would advise you to take the next plane home.' Cripps replied, 'I will consider that.'"

"What is your criticism of the Cripps offer?" I inquired. "Didn't it promise you dominion status with the right to secede from the British Commonwealth?"

"C. F. Andrews [*Manchester Guardian* correspondent in India and for years an intimate friend of Gandhi's] always used to assert that dominion status is not for India," Gandhi declared. "We have not the same relation to Britain as the dominions which are white and settled, for the most part, by emigrants from Britain or their descendants. We do not wish any status conferred on us. If a status is conferred on us, it means we are not free. As to secession, there are big flaws. One of the chief flaws is the provision in the Cripps proposal regarding the princes. The British maintain that they must protect the princes under treaties which they forced on the princes for Britain's advantage. The Maharajah of Bikaner, and I take him as any X, Y, Z, reigned before the British came and had more power then than now. The second flaw is the recognition of Pakistan. The differences between Hindus and Moslems have been accentuated by British rule. Now they have been given their maximum scope by the Cripps offer. Lord Minto started this when he was Viceroy [1909] by establishing separate electorates for the two religious communities, and since then the British have sought to divide us still further. Lord Curzon was a great administrator. I never met him as I have met Chelmsford, Irwin [Halifax], and Linlithgow. But he said one thing to one man, another to a second man, and still a third thing to a third man. With Sir Samuel Hoare, I know whom I am talking to. I know where he stands. But not with Curzon. The division of Bengal, as carried out by Curzon, was a necessary reform. It was a good measure. But it had the effect of dividing the province according to religion. Cripps introduced this same principle in his offer; that is the second big flaw. There can be no unity in India, therefore, as long as the British are here."

"Well," I said, "you did not like the outlines of the post-war settlement proposed by Cripps. But was there nothing desirable in the interim or immediate provisions? Did you not think that, irrespective of the plan for the future, there might be some value in the immediate arrangements which would give your people experience in government and earn you the right to demand freedom after the war?"

"Roughly," Gandhi replied, "this was the spirit in which I approached it. But when I saw the text of the Cripps offer, I was certain that there was no room for cooperation. The main issue was defense. In war time, defense is the chief task of government. I have no desire to interfere with the actual conduct of the war. I am incompetent to do so. But Roosevelt has no special training in strategy, or if he has it is partial." He hesitated a moment. "Or, let me take Churchill."

"No," I said, "you needn't hesitate to take Roosevelt as an example. I understand the point."

"The point is," Gandhi asserted, "that in war time there must be civilian control of the military, even though the civilians are not as well trained in strategy as the military. If the British in Burma wish to destroy the golden pagoda because it is a beacon to Japanese airplanes, then I say you cannot destroy it, because when you destroy it you destroy something in the Burmese soul. When the British come and say, we must remove these peasants to build an airdrome here, and the peasants must go today, I say, 'Why did you not think of that yesterday and give the poor people time to go, and why don't you find places for them to go to?' "

"If these are the matters which you wish Indians to control," I suggested, "I am sure General Wavell would have regarded them as interference in the prosecution of the war."

"The British," Gandhi declared with a smile, "offered us wartime tasks like the running of canteens and the printing of stationery, which are of minor significance. Though I am no strategist, there are things we could have done which would have been more conducive to success in the war. The British have fared so badly in the Far East that they could do with help from us."

"Apparently, then," I summarized, "you placed chief stress on defense."

He agreed.

"Did Nehru and other Congress leaders take the same view?"

"I hope so," he replied. "I hope Nehru takes the same view, and that the Maulana Sahib [Maulana Abul Kalam Azad, the Moslem president of the Congress Party] takes the same view."

"In other words," I said, "you found nothing good in the Cripps proposals?"

"I am glad you put this direct and definite question to me," he exclaimed. "No. I found nothing good at all in them."

"Did you tell that to Cripps?" I inquired.

"Yes," he answered. "I said to Cripps, 'You performed a miracle in Russia.' "

"Why did you say that?" I interrupted. "It wasn't Sir Stafford Cripps who brought Russia into the war, but a gentleman named Adolf Hitler."

Gandhi laughed, and his friends laughed. "But I and thousands of Indians," he protested, "believed that it was Cripps who performed the miracle."

"Didn't Cripps protest when you said that?" I asked.

"No," Gandhi said laughingly, "he took the compliment. We thought Stalin had asked for British aid before the invasion of Russia."

"No, that is not correct," I said. "After the invasion, Russia got help and is now obtaining increasing help from America and Britain. But before the attack, Stalin, fearing Hitler, could show no friendship for Britain or for Cripps."

"In any case," Gandhi continued, "I asked Cripps to perform a miracle here too, but it was not in his power."

I said, "I think there is a vast popular ferment going on in England. I flew to England last summer and stayed nine weeks. The mass of the people are resolved not to be ruled after the war by the sort of people who ruled them before the war and brought on this war. Cripps could become the expression and embodiment of this popular protest. His rise to office is therefore an encouraging phenomenon."

"Yes," Gandhi interpolated, "and a discouraging one too, for I wonder whether Cripps has the qualities of a great statesman. It is very discouraging to us that the man who was a friend of Jawaharlal's and had been interested in India should have made himself the bearer of this mission."

Apparently something went through Gandhi's mind—probably that my hour with him was drawing to a close—for he said, apropos of nothing, "Lord Sankey once told me to take care of myself, and I said to him, 'Do you think I would have reached this green old age if I hadn't taken care of myself?' This is one of my faults."

"I thought you were perfect," I said with a smile.

He said, laughing, "No, I am very imperfect. Before you are gone you will have discovered a hundred of my faults, and if you don't I will help you to see them." He looked down at the large nickel watch which hung by a chain from the waistline of his loincloth, and said to me, "Now, I have given you an hour."

I got up, bowed, and left. During the hour, a Moslem woman without teeth had come in once to change the moistened cloth on his chest. He himself had several times taken the kerchief from his head, rolled it up, immersed it in a tumblerful of water, wrung it out, and put it back on his head. Every time he took off the cloth I had a better view of his little face, with its short, black-and-white, but chiefly white, stubble moustache on his narrow upper lip—so narrow in fact that the fat down-pointed nose tip almost meets the lip. His lower lip is very sensitive and expressive. His eyes are soft. The face is the small lower extension of a big, bulging head with large ears extending abruptly away from it.

A few minutes after I returned to the guest house, Dev, the Socialist leader, arrived with a member of the ashram to discuss India and Russia and the war. They were passionately anti-British. Dev said he was sorry that this was so, but India had suffered at the hands of England and their views were an emotional reaction to national suffering.

I wanted to have a complete record of what Gandhi had said to me, and so, after Dev and his friend had left, I took off the jacket of the blue-striped pajama suit which I had worn for the Gandhi interview and settled down to type notes. After five minutes, I was tired and running with perspiration. I took another splash bath in my water room. As I sat on the terrace, typing, I watched a young Indian woman who walked to and fro in front of the house. She was barefooted and wore a tight blue homespun bodice around her breasts and shoulders, leaving a strip bare to the waist. From the waist down to her feet she wore a sari, the train of which she held under one arm and wrapped around her neck and head. The sari was of bright yellow with a broad, bright-red border, so that every time she passed, I, with my eyes on the typewriter, had the impression of a flame. She carried on her head a large red earthen jar filled with water, and supported it with one arm, which was bare except for a bright metal bracelet at the wrist. When she returned a moment later, after having poured the water into a barrel outside the house opposite, the jar was lying on its side, nestling in a round, rag cup on the top of her head. Hour after hour, in the blazing sun, she did this difficult chore. A short pipe would have relieved her of all this hard work.

I wrote until I was exhausted from the heat, and then chatted with Kurshed. Dinner was at five, announced by a soft gong. The meal started with the usual prayer. A member of the ashram who sat near Gandhi and talked with him in Hindustani used an English word. I said that reminded me of the open-air Congress mass meeting I had attended in New Delhi the day after I arrived in India. The main speaker had been Mrs. Asaf Ali (Hindu wife of Dr. Asaf Ali, a Moslem member of the Congress Working Committee). She too had spoken Hindustani, but I had taken down the English words she used. They were: "foreign policy," "exploitation," "social position," "efficiency," "British Imperialism," "non-cooperation," "India Office," and "refugees." Gandhi enjoyed the list immensely. A man sitting near by said there was another English phrase they all knew: "student spies." The government used some university students to spy on others, he said. Gandhi said, "This is one of my indictments of British rule."

Gandhi asked me about the terror in Soviet Russia. I gave him details from my experience in Russia. "Then England and the United States," Gandhi volunteered, "are the only democratic countries left in the world."

"It is surprising," I corroborated, "how democratic England remains despite the war. There is also Sweden."

"Yes?" Gandhi commented incredulously.

"And Switzerland. And the British dominions," I added.

"For whites," Gandhi interjected. "I know. I have lived in South Africa." He returned to his food.

I went back to the hut for a bath. All I had to do to take a bath was to slip off my pajamas and sandals and fill a bowl with water and hold it over my head and tilt it. Refreshed, I made my way again to Gandhi's house at 6.15 P.M. I waited outside a minute until Gandhi came out. He carried a long stick of bamboo. Dr. Das, Gandhi's physician who lives in the ashram, accompanied us and so did several young men and women. Gandhi leaned his hands on the shoulders of two of the women. A group of young men visitors from outside the village had posted themselves not far from Gandhi's house to catch a glimpse of him as he passed. Their faces pictured awe and devotion. They touched palms in front of their lips and bent forward low from the waist. Gandhi made a remark to them which made him and them laugh. A second group of older men, one with a big paunch, looked eagerly as though in the hope of getting a greeting, but failed. We took the dusty road that wound around ploughed fields. Gandhi invited questions from me with a "Now?"

"You helped recruit soldiers for the British Army in the first World War," I began. "When this war started, you said you wished to do nothing to embarrass the British government. Now, obviously, your attitude has changed. What has happened?"

"In the first World War I had just returned from South Africa," he explained. "I hadn't yet found my feet. I wasn't sure of my ground. This did not imply any lack of faith in non-violence. But it had to develop according to circumstances, and I was not sufficiently sure of my ground.

There were many experiences between the two wars. Nevertheless, I announced after some talks with the Viceroy in September, 1939, that the Congress movement would not obstruct this war. I am not the Congress. In fact, I am not in the Congress. I am neither a member nor an officer of the Party. Congress is more anti-British and anti-war than I am, and I have had to curb its desires to interfere with the war effort. Now I have reached certain conclusions. I do not wish to humiliate the British. But the British must go. I do not say that the British are worse than the Japanese."

"Quite the contrary," I interjected.

"I would not say quite the contrary," he rejoined. "But I do not wish to exchange one master for another. England will benefit morally if she withdraws voluntarily and in good order."

Gandhi then talked at length and scarcely stopping for breath—although we were walking at a fast pace and it was still hot—about what he called British atrocities in Bengal and elsewhere. He said he had received letters only today telling how villagers were being driven from their homes without notice and without compensation in order to make way for the construction of airdromes. "This," he commented, "impedes the war effort, although it appears to be part of the war effort. I am more than ever convinced that Britain cannot win this war unless she leaves India."

It was dark when we returned to Gandhi's house. He lay down on one of the wooden beds in the courtyard, and asked me to sit down on one near by. The Moslem woman brought him a dry chest cloth and then proceeded to wipe his feet. I expressed the view that England might have made mistakes in India and engaged in repression at times, but that a foreign dictatorship which conquered the country would be infinitely worse. In reply, he talked at length and with bitterness about the Amritsar Massacre in 1919 and other violent British acts in India. He insisted that he was more moderate than the people and that some Indians were so anti-British they would not mind the victory of Japan.

He made a move to get up, and I said it was time for me to go. He said, "No, come to prayers."

It was now black night. I followed Gandhi to an open spot about fifty yards from his house, where the members of the ashram, about seventy in all, mostly dressed in white, squatted on the ground on three sides of a square. The women were on the left side of the square, and the men on the two other sides. Gandhi said, "Fischer, can you squat here?" and I sat down next to where he had taken his position in the center of the fourth side of the square, with his face to the congregation. The Moslem woman sat behind him and fanned him with a straw fan. Some of the worshippers had kerosene lanterns which were shaded with paper on one side so that the light would not shine into the eyes of persons opposite. One such lamp stood at Gandhi's side. The prayer meeting started when Gandhi commenced to recite a verse. All joined in the chant, and he kept pace with them and his voice sounded clearly above all the rest. Then a song leader started to sing, and a man beside him beat tiny metal cymbals and everybody sang a sort of wailing song which sounded part Chinese, part a falsetto, monotone Arabic. Later Gandhi read from a thick volume of Hindu scriptures. A prayer for peace ended the services.

June 5, 1942

I was up at four, after a refreshing night under
the stars and moon. I slept on a bed made of rope
netting attached to four wooden posts. The air
during the night was cool. At six-fifteen, Dr. Das,
my neighbor, came and said that Gandhi was tired
and would not walk this morning. Kurshed
brought me a breakfast of tea with biscuits, butter,
honey, and mangoes. I ate quickly while flies and
ants competed with me. After breakfast I typed
notes but interrupted when Dev and Aryanaikam,
a huge dark Ceylonese who was a leading Congress
educator, came to talk about Russia. I voiced the
view that independence was not enough, and that
after independence India's real headaches would
start. Kurshed repeated her statement of yesterday
that she wanted a free India even if it were fascist.
If Bose (Subhas Chandra Bose, president of Congress in 1938, who escaped from India after the beginning of the war and took up residence in Germany, whence he broadcast against British rule)

entered India at the head of an Indian army, he could rally the whole country. The Japanese, she said, had liberated the Indian soldiers and officers captured in Hong Kong, Malay, Singapore, and Burma and were organizing them into special Indian units which, the Axis radio declared, would march into India and drive out the British. Bose, she said, was more popular than Nehru, and in certain circumstances had a stronger appeal than Gandhi.

Dev stated that, in recent years, under pressure from Nehru and other advanced thinkers, Congress had been paying more attention to economic and social questions, and had formulated a social program which he would find and give me.

Lunch at eleven. I was late in arriving. Gandhi was already seated on the floor of the mess hall. "Come along," he said to me in friendly fashion as I appeared. I asked him whether he was well. "Yes," he replied, "but I felt too tired to walk. You must walk alone or with some of our friends. Exercise is important." I told him that only the chance of talking to him could induce me to walk in this heat. He laughed. He offered me a boiled onion from his pot. I turned it down and asked for raw onion instead. It stimulated my palate and was a relief from the flat food of the menu. Kurshed handed me a teaspoon, but Gandhi pushed a tablespoon in my direction and said, "This is more consistent with your size." When I got to my mango at the end of the meal, he handed me a homespun napkin. I said, "When in Rome I want to do as the Romans do and not be an exception."

"You are," he replied, "and besides I have a napkin too."

At three in the afternoon I walked over to Gandhi's house for my interview. Desai and another secretary were on the floor writing replies to letters received by Gandhi. Kurshed took over the fan. I noticed a second decoration in the room: a dull-colored picture of a religious procession painted on the mud wall of the room. Also, on the wall behind Gandhi's back were shallow reliefs of a palm tree and of a palm leaf on which was inscribed a large figure resembling the Arabic numeral three. This, Desai explained to me, was a religious symbol called "Ohm" which had the same significance as the Greek "logos."

Gandhi came in, greeted me, and lay down on his bed. "I will take your blows lying down," he said. The Moslem woman gave him a wet mudpack for his abdomen. He said, "This puts me in touch with my future." I said nothing, and after a moment he remarked, "I see you missed that one." I told him I hadn't missed it, but thought he was too young to think about returning to the dust.

"Why," he exclaimed, "you and I and all of us, some in a hundred and twenty years, but all sooner or later, will do it." He paused and invited questions with a "Now?"

I said that when I hear a suggestion about some arrangement for the future I try to imagine how it would look if it were actually adopted. "I am sure you have done the same in connection with your proposal that the British withdraw. Then how do you see that withdrawal, step by step?"

"First," he replied with deliberation, "there are the Princes who have their own armies. They might make trouble. I am not sure that there will be order when the British go. There could be chaos. I have said, 'Let the British go in an orderly fashion and leave India to God.' You may not like such unrealistic language. Then call it anarchy. That is the worst that can happen. But we will seek to prevent it. There may not be anarchy."

"Could not the Indians immediately organize a government?" I suggested.

"Yes," he responded quickly. "There are three elements in the political situation here: the Princes, the Moslems, and Congress. They could all form a provisional government."

"In what proportion," I asked, "would power and the posts be divided?"

"I do not know," he replied. "Congress being the most powerful unit might claim the largest share. But that could be determined amicably."

"It seems to me," I said, "that the British cannot

possibly withdraw altogether. That would mean making a present of. India to Japan, and England would never consent to that, nor would the United States approve. If you demand that the British pack up and go bag and baggage, you are simply asking the impossible; you are barking up a tree. You do not mean, do you, that they must also withdraw their armies?"

For at least two minutes Gandhi said nothing. The silence in the room was almost audible. "You are right," he said at last. "No, Britain and America, and other countries too, can keep their armies here and use Indian territory as a base for military operations. I do not wish Japan to win the war. I do not want the Axis to win. But I am sure that Britain cannot win unless the Indian people become free. Britain is weaker and Britain is morally indefensible while she rules India. I do not wish to humiliate England."

"But if India is to be used as a military base by the United Nations, many other things are involved. Armies do not exist in a vacuum. For instance, the United Nations would need good organization on the railroads."

"Oh," he exclaimed, "they could operate the railroads. They would also need order in the ports where they received their supplies. They could not have riots in Bombay and Calcutta. These matters would require cooperation and common effort."

"Could the terms of this collaboration," I urged, "be set forth in a treaty of alliance?"

"Yes," he said, "we could have a written agreement with England."

"Or with Britain, America and the others," I amplified.

He nodded his head in assent.

"Why have you never said this?" I asked. "I must confess that when I heard of your proposed civil disobedience movement I was prejudiced against it. I believed that it would impede the prosecution of the war. I think the war has to be fought and won. I see complete darkness for the world if the Axis wins. I think we have a chance for a better world if we win."

"There I cannot quite agree," he argued. "Britain often cloaks herself in a cloth of hypocrisy, promising what she later doesn't deliver. But I accept the proposition that there is a better chance if the democracies win."

"It depends on the kind of peace we make," I said.

"It depends on what you do during the war," he corrected.

"I would like to tell you," I began, "that American statesmen have great sympathy for the cause of Indian freedom. The United States government tried to dissuade Churchill from making the speech in which he declared that the Atlantic Charter did not apply to India. Important men in Washington are working on the idea of a Pacific Charter, but they tell me that they have not got very far because the first principle of such a charter would be the end of imperialism, and how can we announce that while Britain holds India?"

"I am not interested in future promises," he asserted. "I am not interested in independence after the war. I want independence now. That will help England win the war."

"Why have you not communicated your plan to the Viceroy?" I asked. "He should be told that you have no objection now to the use of India as a base for Allied military operations."

"No one has asked me," Gandhi replied. "I have written about my proposed civil disobedience movement in order to prepare the public for it. If you put me some direct questions in writing about this matter, I will answer them in *Harijan* [Gandhi's English-language weekly magazine. "Harijan" means "Untouchable"]. Only make the questions brief."

"If you knew anything about my writing you would know," I preached, "that I always try to be brief, direct, and squeeze out all the water."

"Jawaharlal told me about you before you

came," Gandhi said. "He said you were honest and had no axe to grind. You don't have several irons in the fire. He said you were a solid man. I can see that by looking at you," he laughed.

"Yes, solid, at least physically," I said.

"I have talked freely and frankly to you," he declared. "I think you are a sahib loke."

He laughed and I asked for help. "Did you say 'sahib bloke'? Is that the English word bloke?" The whole company roared with laughter.

"No, loke," he laughed. One secretary interpreted it as meaning "two gentlemen." Mahadev Desai, sitting there with a thick mudpack diaper-pinned on his head like a Cossack's cap, said it meant "superfine."

"Miss Katherine Mayo (author of *Mother India*)," Gandhi said when the laughter died down, "came here and I was good to her, and then she wrote only filth. You know what I have called her?"

"No," I said.

"Drain inspector," Gandhi said.

"I come from a very poor family," I said. "I know what it means to be hungry. I have always sympathized with the downtrodden and the poor. Many Americans feel the greatest friendship for India. I think it very unfortunate, therefore, that you have recently uttered some unfriendly words at the expense of America."

"It was necessary," Gandhi affirmed. "I wanted to shock. I think many Americans have a soft corner in their hearts for me, and I wished to tell them that if they continue to worship/Mammon they will not make a better world. There is a danger that the democracies will defeat the Axis and become just as bad as Japan and Germany."/

"Of course there is a danger," I broke in. "But many people said that England would go fascist if it went to war. Yet in fact England is more democratic now than she was before the war."

"No," he disagreed. "We see in India that this is not so."

"At least in England," I suggested.

"It cannot be true in England," Gandhi insisted, "and not in the Empire. I cannot depend on your future goodness. I have labored for many decades for Indian national freedom. We cannot wait any longer. But I believe that there is good will for us."

He paused, and I thought he looked very disconsolate. "England," he said with deliberation, "is sitting on an unexploded mine in India and it may explode any day. The hatred and resentment against Britain are so strong here that Britain can get no help for her war effort. Indians enlist in the British Army because they want to eat, but they have no feeling in their hearts which would make them wish to help England."

"If you permit me to summarize the suggestions you have made today about a settlement in India," I said, "you have reversed the Cripps offer. Cripps offered you something and kept the rest for England. You are offering England something and keep the rest for India."

"That is very true," he agreed. "I have turned Cripps around."

I saw from his watch that the end of the hour was approaching. I said I would not dare ask him to read my book, *Men and Politics,* which Dev had, but I hoped he would page through it. A secretary asked what "paging through" meant. Gandhi said, "It means looking first at the last page, then at the first page, then at a page in the middle."

"And then throwing the book away and saying it is excellent," I suggested. "Now I have kept you the agreed hour."

"Yes, you have," he said. "Go and sit in the tub."

As I walked out of the house, I thought to myself, is that the Indian equivalent of go sit on a tack? But I thought it was a good idea anyway, only I decided to improve on it. When I got home I stripped, placed a small wooden packing case in one of the tin washtubs filled with water, folded a Turkish towel and put it on the packing case, then set a somewhat larger wooden packing case just outside the tub and put my portable typewriter on it. Having made these arrangements, I sat down on the box in the tub and typed my notes of the hour's talk with Gandhi. At intervals of a few minutes, when I began to perspire, I filled a bronze bowl with water from the tub and poured it over my back and limbs. By that method I was able to type for a whole hour without feeling too tired.

Dinner at five. I arrived earlier than Gandhi, and when he came in he said to me, "That's better." This was a reference to my having been late at lunch. I said I didn't know whether it was more polite to come earlier or later than he did. "Artificial politeness," he said, "is taboo here. Come whenever you like."

He again tried to make me take a boiled onion. Again I refused firmly. "You will be famished here," he said. I told him I cheated between meals and had buttermilk and tea. I said I had improved on his suggestion to sit in a tub and read—I sat in a tub and wrote, and I described my method. He laughed loudly. He apologized because he would not walk this evening; he felt tired.

When he saw that I had finished the meal, he said, "Fischer, you can go whenever you please. Don't stand on ceremony. As I told you before, we want no artificial politeness here." I got up, found my hat and shoes, and when I was outside the dining hall he said to me, "Has anyone told you that Jawaharlal is coming here on Sunday?"

"No," I said, "what day is this? I've lost count of the days."

"Friday," he laughed.

"Would you agree," I asked, "to stand for a photograph with me?"

"If a photographer is around by accident," Gandhi replied. "I have no objections to being seen on a photograph with you."

"That," I said, "is the biggest compliment you have paid me."

"Do you want compliments?" he inquired.

"Don't we all?" I said.

"Yes," he agreed, "but sometimes we have to pay too dearly for them."

I went home, got back into the tub, and typed out four questions which Gandhi had promised to answer in *Harijan*.

I felt that my interview with Gandhi today was of historic importance. He had changed his mind on what was the crucial issue for India; instead of his former statement that 'The British Must Go,' he had said to me, 'The British can stay and conduct the war from India.' In other words, he was ready to tolerate the war effort and, under certain circumstances, support it. His statements to me had indicated his readiness to compromise on the vital issue of Indian independence.

I lolled in my bed which stands in the open not far from the guest house. Kurshed warned me not

to step off the bed at night without taking hold of
the lighted kerosene lantern she had placed on the
porch near by; she said scorpions were abroad.

From a distance I heard the soft tones of the
prayer meeting, and then fell asleep at about nine.
The night was cool.

I ROSE at five, shaved, and dressed in the pants of the blue-striped pajama suit I had bought in London and in the home-spun white khadi blouse which Aryanaikam loaned me. It reached to my knees. Breakfast of mangoes, tea, and bread. Then I walked over to Gandhi's hut. He was sitting on his bed outside and ladling spoonfuls of mango from a deep tumbler. His wife fanned him. He wore only a loincloth.

He greeted me with an "Oh" and commented on my costume. I said, "How do you like this combination of Piccadilly and khadi?"

He said it looked fine. "You must have had a special size made for you," he added. I told him I had borrowed it from Aryanaikam. Gandhi said, "You know he studied at Columbia University in America." I said I knew. After a pause, I asked him whether he had seen my questions. He said, "Yes, I will tackle them this morning."

Soon after we started on the morning walk, I

asked him what was the theory behind his weekly day of silence. "What do you mean by theory?" he asked.

"I mean the principle, the motivation," I replied.

He smiled. "It happened when I was being torn to pieces," he began. "I was working very hard, travelling in hot trains incessantly, speaking at many meetings, and being approached in trains and elsewhere by thousands of people who asked questions, made pleas, and wished to pray with me. I wanted to rest for one day a week. So I instituted the day of silence. Later of course I clothed it with all kinds of virtues and gave it a spiritual cloak. But the motivation was really nothing more than that I wanted to have a day off."

We walked on. He leaned his hand on a young woman who worked in the ashram kitchen. "Silence is very relaxing," he mused. "It is not relaxing in itself. But when you can talk and don't, it gives you great relief—and there is time for thought."

I was walking next to Gandhi but the girl from the kitchen had interposed a big black umbrella between us to keep the sun off Gandhi. He wore no cloth on his chest or head. Dr. Das came up and shaded Gandhi with an umbrella from the other side. At times, Dr. Das hurried ahead and removed long bamboo sticks from the road and threw them into the fields.

I asked Gandhi for his opinion about the proposals of C. Rajagopalachari, who had participated, as Congress representative, in the negotiations with Sir Stafford Cripps in April. Rajaji, as the Indians call him, is one of the wisest men in India, an old friend and associate of Gandhi's, and the father of the wife of Gandhi's youngest son, Devadas. Ever since the failure of the Cripps proposals, Rajaji had been making many speeches urging the Congress Party and the Moslem League to get together on the basis of a Congress acceptance of Pakistan—a separate Moslem state. When I asked Gandhi about Rajaji's program, he said, "I don't know what his proposals are. I think it unfortunate that he should argue against me and that I should argue with him, so I have given order that, as far as we are concerned, the discussion should be suspended. But the fact is that I do not know what Rajaji proposes."

"Isn't the essence of his scheme," I asked, "that the Hindus and Moslems collaborate and in common work perhaps discover the technique of peaceful cooperation?"

"Yes," Gandhi replied, "but that is impossible. As long as the third power, England, is here, our communal differences will continue to plague us.

Far back, Lord Minto, then Viceroy, declared that
the British had to keep Moslems and Hindus apart
in order to facilitate the domination of India."

I told Gandhi I had seen that Minto quotation.
"This has been the principle of British rule ever
since," Gandhi emphasized.

"I have been told," I said, "that when Congress
ministries were in office in the provinces, during
1937, 1938, and 1939, they discriminated against
Moslems."

"The British governors of those provinces have
officially testified that that is not so," Gandhi asserted sharply.

"But isn't it a fact," I persisted, "that in the
United Provinces, Congress and the Moslems entered into an electoral pact because Congress was
not sure of winning, that, then, Congress won a
sweeping victory and refused to form a coalition
with the Moslems?"

"No," Gandhi contradicted. "There were four
Moslem ministers in the United Provinces government formed by Congress. There were no representatives of the Moslem League, but there were
Moslems. No. We have always tried to collaborate
with Moslems. It is said that the Maulana [Mau-
lana Abul Kalam Azad, President of the Congress,
is a Moslem scholar] is a puppet in our hands. Actually, he is the dictator of Congress. He is its
president. But the Cripps proposals have divided

Hindus from Moslems more than ever. Thanks to the British government, the divergence between the two communities has been widened."

"It was sad," I volunteered, "that Congress leaders and Moslem Leaguers came to New Delhi to talk to Cripps, and talked to Cripps but did not talk to one another."

"It was not only sad," Gandhi agreed, "it was disgraceful. But it was the fault of the Moslem League. Shortly after this war broke out, we were summoned to meet the Viceroy at New Delhi. Rajendra Prasad [a member of the Congress Working Committee] and I went to speak for Congress, and Mr. Jinnah for the Moslem League. I asked Jinnah to confer with us in advance and face the British government unitedly. We agreed to meet in New Delhi, but when I suggested that we both demand independence for India he said, 'I do not want independence.' We could not agree. I urged that we at least make the appearance of unity by going to the Viceroy together; I said he could go in my car or I would go in his. He consented to have me go in his car. But we spoke to the Viceroy in different tones and expressed different views."

By this time, we had returned to Gandhi's house. He stopped outside. I leaned against one of the bamboo supports of the house to rest, but Gandhi carried on full of pep. "In actual life," he insisted, "it is impossible to separate us into two nations. We are not two nations. Every Moslem will have a Hindu name if he goes back far enough in his family history. Every Moslem is merely a Hindu who has accepted Islam. That does not create nationality. If some influential Christian divine converted us all to Christianity, we should not become one nation if we really were two nations, and in the same manner the two religions of India do not make two nationalities. Europe is Christian, but Germany and England, so much alike in culture and language, are grimly at one another's throats. We in India have a common culture. In the north, Hindi and Urdu are understood by both Hindus and Moslems. In Madras, Hindus and Moslems speak Tamil, and in Bengal they both speak Bengali and neither Hindi nor Urdu. When communal riots take place, they are always provoked by incidents over cows and by religious processions. That means that it is our superstitions that create the trouble and not our separate nationalities."

"Caroe [the Viceroy's Secretary for Foreign Affairs who worked for many years as a British official in the Punjab] and Jenkins [a high British official in the Department of Supplies]," I said, "told me that there were no communal differences in the villages, and I heard from others too that the relations between the two religious communities are peaceful in the villages. If that is so, that is very important because India is ninety per cent village."

"It is so," Gandhi stated, "and that of course proves that the people are not divided. It proves that the politicians divide us."

I told Gandhi that the Moslem bartender in my hotel in New Delhi said to me—although he is a member of the Moslem League and an advocate of Pakistan—that the communal troubles always started where Moslems were a minority and never where the Hindus were a minority. "Fischer," Gandhi explained, "you have been here only for a short time. You cannot study everything. But if you make any investigations and find that we are wrong or guilty, please say so in a loud voice."

He had walked me over to a long building made of bamboo. "These are my patients," he said. He stopped at a bed on which a woman was sitting. She seemed ill. Gandhi talked to her for about five minutes and she laughed and he laughed all the time. "She is one of my best patients," Gandhi declared.

Dr. Das was with us. I said, in order to provoke Gandhi, "Wouldn't it be better to leave her to the doctor?"

"No," Gandhi replied, "there is much quackery in all this." Then he went into a room which was empty but for a red wooden cradle. The mother took the baby out of the cradle as Gandhi entered.

He smacked the baby's cheeks as he said, "She is not my patient, she is my relaxation." The baby reacted gleefully and he smacked and pinched it some more. Gandhi said, "This baby's father was a sergeant in the British Army stationed at the Northwest Frontier. He was ordered to shoot at Indians. He refused and was sentenced to sixteen years' imprisonment. He served six years, but there were so many petitions for his liberation that he was released two years ago. Now he lives here with us." We walked back to Gandhi's house, and I left him.

On my way home I stopped at the house opposite mine where one of Gandhi's secretaries lives. During my interviews with Gandhi, he has sat nearest Gandhi. He is short and dark with an intense face. He has worked with Gandhi for twenty-four years. I asked him what he thought of Gandhi's statements to me yesterday about allowing the British to remain in India. He said it was very interesting "and very new and much of a shock. I do not believe that any good can come of war. We must not collaborate in any war." He repeated these statements several times. This was frank criticism of his saintly chief. It did not indicate that Gandhi's intimate associates were terrorized by him. I later asked the name of this secretary. It is Kishorlal Ghaneshyamlal Masruwala. The middle name is the name of a god.

I typed in the tub until lunchtime.

At lunch Gandhi said, "Fischer, give me your bowl and I will give you some vegetables." I told him I had eaten the mess of squash and spinach four times in two days and had no desire for more. He said, "You don't like vegetables?"

"I don't like the taste of these vegetables," I replied.

"Ah," he exclaimed, "you must add plenty of salt and lemon."

"You want me to kill the taste," I suggested.

"No," he replied laughingly, "enrich the taste."

"You are so non-violent," I said. "You wouldn't even kill a taste."

"If that were the only thing men killed, I wouldn't mind," he replied.

I perspired and wiped my face and neck with a handkerchief. I turned to Gandhi and said, "Next time I am in India . . ." He was chewing and didn't seem to pay any attention, so I stopped.

Without turning his head to me, Gandhi said, "Yes, the next time you are in India . . . ?"

"You either ought to have air-conditioning in Sevagram," I continued, "or live in the Viceroy's palace."

"All right," he said as though he meant it.

I slept after lunch, then recorded my morning talk with Gandhi and later read from the lengthy report of the Simon Indian Statutory Commission, which was presented to Parliament in May, 1930. On page 59 of Volume I, this passage occurs: "There is among the Hindu minority in Sind a feeling that the independence of the [British] Commissioner is too great, while on the Muhammadan side there is a well-known cry for separation from Bombay. This demand has gathered strength not so much in the homes of the people or among the Muhammadan cultivators of Sind, as among the leaders of Muhammadan thought all over India to whom the idea of a new Moslem province, contiguous to the predominantly Moslem areas of Baluchistan, the Northwest Frontier Province, and the Punjab, naturally appeals as offering a stronghold against the fear of Hindu domination."

I began my interview with Gandhi this afternoon by reading this passage to him. I said it confirmed his statement to me this morning that the Moslem people are much less interested in separatism than their leaders.

"Of course," he acquiesced.

"But," I went on, "how real are the fears of the Moslem leaders? Perhaps they understand better than the Moslem masses that the Hindus desire to dominate. Can you say quite objectively that the Hindus have not tried to gain the upper hand?"

"Here and there," Gandhi said, "individuals may entertain regrettable ideas. But I can say that the Congress movement and the Hindus in general have no desire to control. The provinces must enjoy broad autonomy. I myself am opposed to violence or domination and do not believe in powerful governments which oppress their citizens or other states. So how could I wish for domination? This charge is a cry originated by leaders to obtain a better hold on their people."

I said I had several questions to ask him about the Congress Party. Very highly placed Britishers, I recalled, had told me that Congress was in the hands of big business and that Gandhi was supported by the Bombay mill owners who gave him as much money as he wanted. "What truth is there in these assertions?" I asked.

"Unfortunately, they are true," he declared simply. "Congress hasn't enough money to conduct its work. We thought in the beginning to collect four annas [about eight cents] from each member per year and operate on that. But it hasn't worked."

"What proportion of the Congress budget," I asked, "is covered by rich Indians?"

"Practically all of it," he stated. "In this ashram, for instance, we could live much more poorly than we do and spend less money. But we do not, and the money comes from our rich friends."

"Doesn't the fact that Congress gets its money

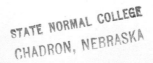

from the moneyed interests affect Congress politics?" I asked. "Doesn't it create a kind of moral obligation?"

"It creates a silent debt," he said. "But actually we are very little influenced by the thinking of the rich. They are sometimes afraid of our demand for full independence."

"The other day," I said, "I noticed in the *Hindustan Times* an item to the effect that Mr. Birla had again raised wages in his textile mills to meet the higher cost of living and, the paper continued to say, no other mill owner had done so much. The *Hindustan Times* is a Congress paper."

"No," Gandhi demurred, "it is completely owned by Birla." He laughed. "I know," he proceeded, "because my youngest son is the editor. The facts are true, but it has nothing to do with Congress. You are right, however, that the dependence of Congress on rich sponsors is unfortunate. I use the word 'unfortunate.' It does not pervert our policy."

"Isn't one of the results," I asked, "that there is a concentration on nationalism almost to the exclusion of social and economic problems?"

"No," he said, "Congress has from time to time, especially under the influence of Pandit Nehru, adopted advanced social programs and schemes for economic planning. I will have those collected for you."

"But is it not a fact," I persisted, "that all these social changes are projected to a time when independence will have been achieved?"

"No," he differed. "When Congress was in office in the Provinces [1937-1939] the Congress ministries introduced many reforms which have since been canceled by the British administration. We introduced reforms in the villages, in the schools, and in other fields."

"I have been told, and I read in the Simon report," I said, "that one of the great curses of India is the village money-lender to whom the peasant is often in debt from birth to death. In European countries, private philanthropy and governments have in similar circumstances created land banks to oust the usurious money-lender. Why could not some of your rich friends start a land bank on a purely business basis except that, instead of getting forty to seventy per cent interest per year, they would get two or three per cent? Their money would be secure, they would earn a small profit, and they would be helping their country."

"Impossible," Gandhi affirmed. "It could not be done without government legislation."

"Why?" I demanded.

"Because the peasants wouldn't repay the loans," he said.

"But surely," I argued, "the peasant would realize that it was better to repay money which he borrowed at three per cent than to mortgage his life away to the money-lender?"

"Money-lending is an ancient institution," he explained, "and it is deeply rooted in the village. What you advocate cannot be done before we are free."

"What would happen in a free India?" I asked. "What is your program for the improvement of the lot of the peasantry?"

"The peasants would take the land," he replied. "We would not have to tell them to take it. They would take it."

"Would the landlords be compensated?" I asked.

"No," he said. "That would be fiscally impossible. You see," he smiled, "our gratitude to our millionaire friends does not prevent us from saying such things. The village would become a self-governing unit living its own life."

"But there would of course be a national government, I said.

"No," he said.

"But surely you need a national administration to direct the railroads, the telegraphs, and so on," I insisted.

"I would not shed a tear if there were no railroads in India," he replied.

"But that would bring suffering to the peasant,"

I said. "He needs city goods, and he must sell his produce in other parts of the country and abroad. The village needs electricity and irrigation. No single village could build a hydro-electric power station or an irrigation system like the Sukkhur barrage in Sind."

"And that has been a big disappointment," Gandhi interjected. "It has put the whole Province in debt."

"I know," I said, "but it has brought much new land under cultivation, and it is a boon to the people."

"I realize," Gandhi said, shaking his head, "that despite my views there will be a central government administration. However, I do not believe in the accepted Western form of democracy with its universal voting for parliamentary representatives."

I was eager to pursue this discussion. "What would you have India do?" I asked.

"There are seven hundred thousand villages in India. Each would be organized according to the will of its citizens, all of them voting. Then there would be seven hundred thousand votes and not four hundred million. Each village, in other words, would have one vote. The villages would elect their district administrations, and the district administrations would elect the provincial administrations, and these in turn would elect a president who would be the national chief executive."

"That is very much like the Soviet system," I said.

"I did not know that," Gandhi admitted. "I don't mind."

"Now, Mr. Gandhi," I said, "I would like to ask you a second question about Congress. Congress has been accused of being an authoritarian organization. There is a new book out by two British authors, Shuster and Wint, called *India and Democracy,* which makes the charge that when the Congress provincial ministries resigned in 1939 they did so not of their own volition but on the orders of the district dictators of Congress."

"This is nonsense," Gandhi said emphatically. "Do you think all questions are decided in the House of Commons or are decisions taken in party caucuses and in the clubs of London? Congress officers are elected by the members of Congress, and ministers who are members of Congress abide by the principles of Congress. Sir Samuel Hoare has told me a few things about the workings of democracy in Britain."

"He seems to be your favorite British statesman," I interjected. This provided much laughter.

"At least," Gandhi said, "I always know where

he stands. Parliamentary democracy is not immune to corruption, as you who remember Tammany Hall and the Mayor of Chicago should know. I do not think a free India will function like the other countries of the world. We have our own forms to contribute."

I said I would like to talk to him for a few moments about Subhas Chandra Bose, the Indian leader who had escaped to Axis territory. I told Gandhi that I was rather shocked when I heard that he had sent a telegram of condolence to Bose's mother on the receipt of the report, since proved false, that Bose had died in an airplane accident.

"Do you mean," Gandhi asked, "because I had responded to news that proved to be false?"

"No," I said, "but that you regretted the passing of a man who went to Fascist Germany and identified himself with it."

"I did it," Gandhi asserted, "because I regard Bose as a patriot of patriots. He may be misguided. I think he is misguided. I have often opposed Bose. Twice I kept him from becoming president of Congress. Finally he did become president, although my views often differed from his. But suppose he had gone to Russia or to America to ask aid for India. Would that have made it better?"

"Yes, of course," I said. "It does make a difference to whom you go."

"I do not want help from anybody to make India free," Gandhi declared. "I want India to save herself."

"Throughout history," I recalled, "nations and individuals have helped foreign countries. Lafayette went from France to assist America in winning independence from Britain. Thousands of Americans and other foreigners died in Spain to save the Spanish Republic."

"Individuals, yes," Gandhi said. "But America is the ally of the England which enslaves us. And I am not yet certain that the democracies will make a better world when they defeat the Fascists. They may become very much like the Fascists themselves."

I said, "This is where, as I told you the other day, we must agree to differ. I find the concentration of Indians on problems of their freedom to the exclusion of social problems a disappointment and a shortcoming. Bose is a young man with a propensity for dramatic action, and were he to succumb in Germany to the lure of Fascism and return to India and make India free but Fascist, I think you would be worse off than under British rule."

"There are powerful elements of Fascism in British rule," Gandhi exclaimed, "and in India these are the elements which we see and feel every day. If the British wish to document their right to win the war and make the world better, they must purify themselves by surrendering power in India. Your President," Gandhi continued with a low voice, "talks about the Four Freedoms. Do they include the freedom to be free? We are asked to fight for democracy in Germany, Italy, and Japan. How can we when we haven't got it ourselves?"

At this point Chaplin of the International News Service and Belden of *Time* and *Life,* who had spent several years in China and had recently trekked out of Burma with General Stilwell, entered the hut in shirts, shorts, and shoes, to interview Gandhi by appointment. Gandhi said I could stay if I wished to listen, and then he turned to them and said, "Can you squat?" When they did so, he said: "One American has been vivisecting me. Now I am at your disposal." He talked to them for half an hour and then I escorted them to my hut, served them cold water, and insisted that they take a splash bath in my water room.

During the afternoon, Mahadev Desai, apparently Gandhi's most important secretary, brought me Gandhi's replies to the questions I submitted to him yesterday at his request. The replies were typed on two long sheets of white paper with corrections in Gandhi's own hand.

My questions to Gandhi were contained in the following letter.

DEAR MR. GANDHI:

On the basis of our conversations these last few days I take the liberty of placing the following questions before you in the hope of receiving your full replies:

1. You ask the British government to withdraw immediately from India. Would Indians thereupon form a national government and what groups or parties would participate in such an Indian government?

2. Would that Indian national government permit the United Nations to use Indian territory as a base of military operations against Japan and other Axis powers?

3. What further assistance would this Indian national government be ready to render the United Nations in the course of the present war against the fascist aggressors?

4. Do you believe this collaboration between India and the Allied powers might or should be formulated in a treaty of alliance or an agreement for mutual aid?

Submitted with profound respect by
LOUIS FISCHER

Gandhi's reply was entitled "Important Questions," and read as follows:

A friend was discussing with us the implications of the new proposal. As the discussion was naturally desultory, I asked him to frame his questions, which

I would answer through *Harijan*. He agreed and gave me the following:

1. *Q.*—You ask the British Government to withdraw immediately from India. Would Indians thereupon form a national government and what groups or parties would participate in such an Indian government?

   A.—My proposal is one-sided, i.e., for the British Government to act upon wholly irrespective of what Indians would do or would not do. I have even assumed temporary chaos on their withdrawal. But if the withdrawal takes place in an orderly manner, it is likely that on their withdrawal a provisional Government will be set up by and from among the present leaders. But another thing may also happen. All those who have no thought of the nation but only of themselves may make a bid for power and get together the turbulent forces with which they would seek to gain control somewhere and somehow. I should hope that with the complete, final and honest withdrawal of the British power, the wise leaders will realize their responsibility, forget their differences for the moment and set up a provisional government out of the material left by the British power. As there would be no power regulating the admission or rejection of parties or persons to or from the council board, restraint alone will be the guide. If that happens probably the Congress, the [Moslem] League and the states representatives will be allowed to function and they will come to a loose understanding on the formation of provisional national government. All this is necessarily guess work and nothing more.

2. *Q.*—Would that Indian national government permit the United Nations to use Indian territory as a base of military operations against Japan and other Axis powers?

A.—Assuming that the national Government is formed and if it answers my expectations, its first act would be to enter into a treaty with the United Nations for defensive operations against aggressive powers, it being common cause that India will have nothing to do with any of the Fascist powers, and India would be morally bound to help the United Nations.

3. *Q.*—What further assistance would this Indian national government be ready to render the United Nations in the course of the present war against the Fascist aggressors?

A.—If I have any hand in guiding the imagined National Government, there would be no further assistance save the toleration of the United Nations on the Indian soil under well-defined conditions. Naturally there will be no prohibition against any Indian giving his own personal help by way of being a recruit or/and of giving financial aid. It should be understood that the Indian army has been disbanded with the withdrawal of British power. Again if I have any say in the councils of the national Government, all its power, prestige and resources would be used towards bringing about world peace. But of course after the formation of the National Government my voice may be a voice in the wilderness and nationalist India may go war-mad.

4. *Q.*—Do you believe this collaboration between India and the Allied powers might or should be formulated in a treaty of alliance or an agreement for mutual aid?

A.—I think the question is altogether premature and in any case it will not much matter whether the relations are regulated by treaty or agreement. I do not even see any difference.

Let me sum up my attitude. One thing and only one thing for me is solid and certain. This unnatural prostration of a great nation—its is neither "nations" nor "peoples"—must cease if the victory of the Allies is to be ensured. They lack the moral basis. I see no difference between the Fascist or Nazi powers and the Allies. All are exploiters, all resort to ruthlessness to the extent required to compass their end. America and Britain are very great nations but their greatness will count as dust before the bar of dumb humanity, whether African or Asiatic. They and they alone have the power to undo the wrong. They have no right to talk of human liberty and all else unless they have washed their hands clean of the pollution. That necessary wash will be their surest insurance of success for they will have the good wishes—unexpressed but no less certain—or millions of dumb Asiatics and Africans. Then but not till then, will they be fight-

ing for a new order. This is the reality. All else is
speculation. I have allowed myself to indulge in it
as a test of my bona fides and for the sake of ex-
plaining in a concrete manner at least what I mean
by my proposal.

M. K. GANDHI.

(These questions and answers appeared in the
Harijan of June 14, 1942.)

At dinner today Gandhi asked me whether I
knew Upton Sinclair. He was interested to know
what Sinclair was doing. He said he now and then
got books written by Sinclair but he had little time
to read. They had corresponded with one another.
He said he thought Sinclair must exercise a salu-
tary influence on American social thinking.

Gandhi watched me eat. Then he said, "You
still refuse my vegetables?"

"I defer to you as a man, a leader, and a statesman," I replied, "but not as a chef." I had been
served this mess of spinach leaves and squash at
every meal I had had at Sevagram, and I was
through with it.

He asked me about my two sons. From that
I concluded that he had been looking into "Men
and Politics." Some cats came in and played under
the table on which the large pots and pans of food
stood. I said to Gandhi, "In 1938 I visited Mr.
Lloyd George at Churt and he told me about you."

"Yes," Gandhi said eagerly, "what did he say?"

"He told me that when you came to Churt you squatted on his couch and just as you got settled a black cat which they had never seen before came in through the window and rested in your lap."

"That's correct," Gandhi said.

"And when you left, Lloyd George declared," I said, "the cat disappeared and didn't come back again."

"Ah," said Gandhi, "that I don't know."

Mr. Lloyd George said," I continued, "that the same cat returned when Miss Slade visited him at Churt."

"That too I don't know," Gandhi said. He spoke highly of Lloyd George. I told him that Lloyd George had offered me a cigar or cigarette and I refused because I didn't smoke, and he offered me alcohol which I also refused because I didn't drink, and then Lloyd George said, "No vices," and I said, "No visible ones," and Lloyd George said with gusto, "Well, I have them all, visible and invisible, and that's why I feel so well at seventy-five." Gandhi laughed long. I then told Gandhi that after I had lunched with Lloyd George we walked back to the parlor through a corridor in which there was an enlarged photograph of General Haig, the British commander-in-chief in France during the first World War. Lloyd George pointed to Haig's boots and said, "Haig was brilliant—down here." Gandhi laughed again. He asked me what Lloyd George thought about Churchill. I said I asked Lloyd George that question when I saw him again in the summer of 1941. I asked him why Churchill had no daring, no readiness for adventure. Lloyd George replied in one word, "Gallipoli." Lloyd George explained that that great misadventure had destroyed Churchill's taste for adventure. Gandhi said he was very much impressed when at the end of his talk with Lloyd George at one in the morning— they had met late in the evening because that was the only time that suited them—Lloyd George brought out the entire working personnel of the house to greet him.

I went to bed at eight, after reading yesterday's newspaper. No one here is much interested in reading newspapers, and there is no radio in Sevagram. Indians—there are exceptions like Nehru— live very much inside their country. The war and the outside world are very far away. This is one of the disservices of British rule; the Indians see England first, and this picture close to their eyes prevents them from seeing the world and the war. I slept long. The night was almost cool and very refreshing. Quarter moon and a very bright Milky Way.

THE PHOTOGRAPHS taken yesterday by Kano
Gandhi, the Mahatma's nephew, did not turn out
because the films were out of date, and so I shaved
again early this morning and walked over to
Gandhi. I again found him scooping mango sauce
out of a deep glass while his wife fanned him. He
asked me how I had slept. I told him I had slept
very well, and asked how he had slept. He said he
usually sleeps from 9:30 to 4:30.

"Without interruption?" I asked.

"No," he replied, "with two or three very brief
interruptions. But I have no trouble falling asleep
again. And then I have half an hour's sleep every
afternoon." I told him that Churchill did the
same. "I hear," he said, "that this is becoming
more and more customary in Europe. Especially
in old age it is very important." I told him that it
had been reported that Roosevelt falls asleep the
moment he gets into bed. Gandhi inquired about
Roosevelt's health and then asked me to describe

67

Mrs. Roosevelt to him. "Then she has an influence on American politics?" he asked. I tried to
explain the progress in social legislation, trade-
union organization, and social thinking which had
taken place under the New Deal. I also stressed
the fact that the American government is financing
foreign governments and financing domestic war
industries. I compared that with the private financing of foreign governments and of American industry during the first World War.

"What about the Negroes?" Gandhi asked.

I talked about the Negro situation in the North
and South. I said I did not, of course, wish to defend the treatment meted out to Negroes, but it
seemed to me that it was not so cruel as untouchability in India.

"As you know," he answered, "I have fought untouchability for many years. We have many untouchables here in the ashram. Most of the work
in the ashram is done by the untouchables, and
any Hindu who comes to Sevagram must accept
food from untouchables and remain in their prox-
imity."

I asked whether the discrimination against untouchables had been somewhat alleviated. "Oh,
yes," he replied, "but it is still very bad." Kurshed
came over and said something in Hindustani
which made him laugh. I asked what it was, and
she told me she had said, "I bow to your feet." I

said it was like the men in Vienna who say, "I kiss your hand," but don't do it. Gandhi laughed. Two young boys appeared as he stood up, and they wriggled into position so that he would lean on them during his walk. There is always quite a competition for this honor. One evening a girl came out from the village to meet our group as we returned from the walk, and she skillfully maneuvered herself to Gandhi's side so that the girl who had been there was forced to surrender her place.

I returned to the subject of untouchability as soon as we had started on the morning promenade. I said, "Very thoughtful and otherwise progressive people, for instance Varadachariar [a member of the Supreme Court of India who is a high-caste Brahmin] have tried to justify it in conversation with me; it seems to arise from the belief in the transmigration of the soul which apparently is part of the Hindu religion."

"Do you believe in the transmigration of the soul?" I asked.

"Of course," he answered quickly. "I cannot admit that the soul dies with the body. When a man's house is blown away, he builds himself another. When his body is taken away, his soul finds another. Nor do I accept the view that when the body is laid in the ground the soul remains suspended somewhere waiting for judgment day when it will be brought to the bar and confronted with its crimes. No, it immediately finds itself a new home."

"This is obviously another form of man's eternal striving for immortality," I ventured. "Does it not all arise from the weak mortal's fear of death? Tolstoy was irreligious until his old age, when he started dreading the end."

"I have no fear of death," Gandhi said with emphasis. "I would regard it with relief and satisfaction. But it is impossible for me to think that that is the end. I have no proof. People have tried to demonstrate that the soul of a dead man finds a new home. I do not think this is capable of proof. But I believe it."

And that was that. I knew this was not a subject for argument, but I felt like stating my view again, so I said, "I think we all seek immortality, only some believe they live in their children or their works and some believe they live in transmuted form in animals, or otherwise. Some men live longer because their works last longer, but I believe that faith in one's immortality, if it is distinct from one's acts, is really fear of death and an attempt to find comfort in an illusion." Gandhi thereupon reiterated his view with much passion and in fine-flowing English prose; he always spoke a rich, fluent English with a British university accent.

I said students had told me that the new generation in India was less inclined to make a distinction between high-caste Hindus and Untouchables, or between Hindus and Moslems, and that they were not much interested in religion.

"The first is correct," he agreed. "But Hinduism is not a religion. The students do not perform religious ceremonies. But Hinduism is life. It is a way of life. Many who do not practice formal religion are nearer to this way of life than some who do." He added that untouchability pained him deeply and he hoped that India's freedom would hasten the solution of the problem of untouchability. This brought him back to his favorite subject. He spoke of "the challenge, for it is a challenge, which I have flung to the British to go. They will be purified if they go and better equipped for the task of making a new world. Otherwise all their professions are a cloak of hypocrisy." By this time we had returned to Gandhi's hut and I bade him farewell.

Narendra Dev, the Socialist leader who lives in an alcove next to Gandhi's room, and Aryanaikam, the huge Ceylonese, came to the guest house again this morning and stayed for a long, heated discussion on Fascism and imperialism. They said they continually encountered British Fascism in India, but had not felt and didn't know much about German Fascism. Yes, the intellectuals knew how dreadful the Nazis were, but the people knew

nothing about it. The people were most impressed
by the sinking of the "Prince of Wales" and the
"Repulse"; the British Navy had always been the
real power behind British rule in India. All of
Britain's military reverses in the Far East had
deeply impressed the people. Aryanaikam said Japanese suicide pilots flew their planes straight into
the British battleships, but the British were inca-
pable of such acts. I told him that the British had
suicide pilots too. He replied he had never heard
of them. I recalled the Swordfish airmen of the
R. A. F. who struck at the "Gneisenau" and the
"Scharnhorst," the two German warships which
had recently made a successful dash through the
English Channel. Those pilots, I explained, did
not hesitate to go on a death errand any more than
the Japanese did. All the armed forces of the world
had their heroes, I said, and there was no indica-
tion that the young fighting men of the democracies were decadent.

At the end of our conversation I summed up by
suggesting that Indian anti-Fascists had to fight on
two fronts, against the Axis powers and against
British imperialism. My visitors, however, argued
that they could not fight on one front, let alone
two. "We have no arms," Dev said, "so we cannot
fight on the anti-Japanese front. The British deliberately keep us unarmed. Moreover it is difficult to
fight on the side of the British who hold us down,

who refuse to arm us, and who refuse to make us free."

Dr. Das's niece has a cute little boy of six who plays around the guest house. He speaks a few words of English. I asked him what language he spoke with his playmates. He said he spoke Bengali. He also can talk Hindi and Gujarati. Most of the little children in the ashram speak two or three languages.

Shortly after Dev and Aryanaikan left, I received a visit from Rajah, a Hindu married to a French woman. He had spent many years in France, and his French was even better than his English. He has a handsome Hollywood face with long sideburns and large, arched eyebrows overhanging burning black eyes. He spoke of the rottenness of France. He was spending several months at the ashram to renew his spirit. He had been raised among Moslems in India and had attended a Moslem school. He said the Moslems were more virile than the Hindus and more dynamic, more revolutionary—half the Indian Communist Party, he said, is Moslem. India's best poets are Moslem. The Hindus, he said, are docile and less imaginative. I asked why, since there was no racial difference between Hindus and Moslems, there could be such a divergence of personal characteristics. "Is it food?" I asked. He attributed it to a different outlook on life. The Moslems have a real *joie de vivre.* It wasn't food. In north India many Hindus eat meat. Moslems do not eat pork, but eat beef. "The Hindu," he said, "is contemplative, has a good memory, is a good businessman. But if you want to have a good time and eat well and dance and swim," he advised me, "find a Moslem."

At lunch, Gandhi was in a very jolly mood. He came into the mess hall and made eyes at the two enchanting boys, aged about two and three, who sat on the floor near the entrance patiently waiting for their food. Before he sat down, Gandhi joked with every person he passed and brought them to laughter or smiles. After we had started eating he asked me whether I knew Dr. Kellogg of Battle Creek, Michigan. I said I knew the Kellogg Food Company, but not Dr. Kellogg. Gandhi recalled having corresponded with Dr. Kellogg about dietary questions. "But it often happens," Gandhi said, "that men are better known abroad than at home. There was a dietician named Kuhne in Leipzig whose books had been translated many years ago from German into Indian languages, and had gone into hundreds of editions. But when I sent a friend to look up Kuhne in Leipzig nobody knew about him and it was only after considerable difficulty that the man's son was discovered. Kuhne himself had died."

Gandhi asked me whether I got enough food at the ashram. I said I was never hungry, but that I missed variety in the diet, and that the eye and the sense of taste were very important in eating. "All the meals I have had here have been exactly alike in every detail," I protested. "I am going to attack you publicly as a cook."

Just then Jawaharlal Nehru, dressed in white homespun, a beautiful, smiling figure, entered the dining hall. One could immediately see how much everybody loved him. He sat down on the ground next to me and started eating his food with his fingers, Indian-fashion. I could not help thinking back to a meal we took together in one of the fashionable restaurants of Paris.

Nehru had had a short talk with Gandhi before lunch. After a moment, Gandhi turned to me and said that since he wanted to be able to talk to Jawaharlal tomorrow, Monday, he had planned to change his day of silence and, instead of observing it all day Monday, to go into silence at noon today. But since that would have deprived me of my regular hourly interview this afternoon, he would delay the beginning of the silence until 2:40 this afternoon and talk to me from 1:30 to 2:30.

After lunch Nehru and I sat on two beds in the guest house where he too was staying and talked about everything on earth for about an hour. In one connection he said, "India contains all that is disgusting and all that is noble. You take your choice."

"No," I said, "you take both."

Nehru left me at about twelve-thirty for an hour's talk with Gandhi. When I arrived at Gandhi's hut for my interview, Nehru was there on the floor. He looked unhappy. I sat down next to him. Gandhi turned to me and invited questions with the customary "now?"

I began the interview by commenting on the fact that whereas British law and British political practice required a high centralization of power in Parliament and the Crown, the American political concept was based on the principle of federation. "Don't you think," I asked, "that in view of the diversities of India you will need here a federation which will satisfy the Princes and the Moslems?"

"I am in no position," he confessed, "to say which system would suit us better. First, the British must go. It is a matter of pure speculation what we will do later. The moment the British withdraw, the question of religious minorities disappears. If the British withdraw and there is chaos, I cannot say what form will ultimately rise out of the chaos. If I were asked what I would prefer, I would say federation and not centralization. There is bound to be a federal system of some sort. But you must be satisfied with my answer that I am not disturbed by the problem of whether we are to have a federation or not. Perhaps your cast-iron mind mocks at this. Perhaps you think that with millions unarmed and accustomed to foreign rule for centuries, we will not succeed in the civil disobedience movement which I have decided to launch."

"No," I differed, "I do not think that. I believe that history is moving fast and that before long you will be an independent country like China. The struggle you began years ago cannot end in any other way."

"I do not want to be independent like China," he said with great stress. "China is helpless even now and in spite of Chiang Kai-shek. Notwithstanding China's heroism and her readiness to risk all in this war, China is not yet completely free. China should be able to say to America and England, 'We will fight our battle of independence single-handed, without your aid.' That I would call independence."

I asked him how he got on in his long interview with Chiang. "Very well," he replied.

"Only you did not understand him," I smiled, "and he did not understand you."

"I found him inscrutable," Gandhi admitted. "Maybe it was the matter of language. We spoke through Madame Chiang. But I do not think it was only that."

"Of course China is not completely free," I said, reverting to the subject, "but freedom does not come in a day. Through this war, if we win it,

China will become free. We may be approaching the Asiatic century. India and China may shape a great deal of history in the coming decades. I see no sign, however, that the British realize this. They will not go as you ask. If they could not save themselves by their arms in Singapore and Malay, they will not save themselves by their brains in India."

"I would like you to understand that I am not criticizing China," he affirmed. "Only I wanted to emphasize that I do not wish to imitate China. I do not want India to be in the same predicament as China. That is why I am saying I do not want British and American soldiers here. I do not want Japanese or German soldiers here. The Japanese broadcast every day that they do not intend to keep India—they only propose to help us win our freedom. I do not welcome their sympathy or help. I know they are not philanthropists. I want for India a respite from all foreign domination. I have become impatient. I cannot wait any longer. Our condition is worse than China's or Persia's. I may not be able to convince Congress. Men who have held office in Congress may not rise to the occasion. [Gandhi looked pointedly at Nehru when he said this.] I will go ahead nevertheless and address myself directly to the people. But whatever happens, we are unbendable. We may be able to

evolve a new order which will astonish the whole
world. I would ask you to cast off your prejudices
and enter into this new idea of mine of a civil disobedience campaign and try to find flaws in it if
there are any. [It seemed to me he was talking to
Nehru although directing his words to me, and it
was obvious that Gandhi and Nehru had not seen
eye to eye in their discussion today.] You will
then be able to help our cause, and, to put it on a
higher plane, you will be able to do justice to yourself as a writer. The literature that is being pro-
duced on India is piffling and of no consequence.
There is nothing original in most of it. It is all
cast-iron. I ask you to struggle out of that groove.
I would like you to penetrate through my language
to what I am attempting to express. That is difficult, I know; you came here with all the glamor,
brilliance, culture, and armed strength of American and British civilization. I would understand
your refusing to grasp anything that does not fit
into your groove or that is not desirable for that
groove. But if your mind cannot rise above that
beaten track, then your days in Sevagram will have
been wasted."

"Yes," I said, after a pause during which I tried
to separate what was meant for me and what for
Nehru, "but will you help me to see the new order
you speak of? I am not so sure of my own new or-

der as to reject yours out of hand. I think India has much to contribute, but how do you see future developments?"

"You see," Gandhi began, "the center of power now is in New Delhi, or in Calcutta and Bombay, in the big cities. I would have it distributed among the seven hundred thousand villages of India. That will mean that there is no power. In other words, I want the seven hundred thousand dollars now invested in the imperial bank of England withdrawn and distributed among the seven hundred thousand villages. Then each village will have its one dollar which cannot be lost.

"The seven hundred thousand dollars invested in the imperial bank of India," Gandhi continued, "could be swept away by a bomb from a Japanese plane, whereas if they were distributed among the seven hundred thousand shareholders, nobody could deprive them of their assets. There will then be voluntary cooperation between these seven hundred thousand units, voluntary cooperation—not cooperation induced by Nazi methods. Voluntary cooperation will produce real freedom and a new order vastly superior to the new order in Soviet Russia. Some say there is ruthlessness in Russia but that it is exercised for the lowest and the poorest and is good for that reason. For me it has very little good in it. Some day this ruthlessness will create an anarchy worse than we have ever seen.

I am sure we will escape that anarchy here. I admit that the future society of India is largely beyond my grasp. But a system like the one I have outlined to you did exist though it undoubtedly had its weakness, else it would not have succumbed before the Moghuls and the British. I would like to think that parts of it have survived, and that the roots have survived despite the ravages of British rule. Those roots and the stock are waiting to sprout if a few drops of rain fall in the form of a transfer of British power to Indians. What the plant will be like I do not know. But it will be infinitely superior to anything we have now. Unfortunately, the requisite mood of non-violence does not now exist here, but I refuse to believe that all the strenuous work of the last twenty-five years to evolve a new order has been in vain. The Congress Party will have an effective influence in shaping the new order, and the Moslem League will also have an effective influence."

"I would like you to pursue this idea of the symbolic seven hundred thousand dollars," I suggested. "What will the villages do with the dollar that has come back to them from the imperial bank of England?" I asked.

"One thing will happen," Gandhi asserted. "Today the shareholders get no return. Intermediaries take it away. If the peasants are masters of their dollars they will use them as they think best."

"A peasant buries his money in the ground," I suggested.

"They will not bury their dollars in the ground," Gandhi said, "because they will have to live. They will go back to the bank, their own bank, and utilize it under their direction for purposes they think best. They may then build windmills or produce electricity or whatever they like. A central government will evolve, but it will act according to the wishes of the people and will be broadbased on their will."

"The state, I imagine," I said, "will then build more industries and develop the country industrially."

"You must visualize a central government without the British Army," Gandhi said. "If it holds together without that army, this will be the new order. That is a goal worth working for. It is not an unearthly goal. It is practicable."

"I agree," I said. "Ten years ago I might not have agreed, but after my experiences in Russia and elsewhere I feel that the greatest danger the world faces is the emergence of the all-powerful state which makes individual freedom impossible. Apparently, capitalist economics have made it necessary for the state to intervene more and more in economic affairs. That gives the state more power. The next generation's real problem will be to devise checks and balances on such a state. One question is: Can we safeguard personal liberty in a country where the government is all-powerful? Another question is: Will nations cooperate inside an international organization, or will we reject internationalism and have some more wars?"

"My question would be," Gandhi said, "how to prevent the rise of these gigantic states. That is why I do not want the Allied powers to assume the roles of Fascist states. It is therefore that I ask them to declare that what India says is good. Let us take this jump and give India her freedom, and if necessary remain in India on India's terms for the duration. Let us see if we can get a free cooperation among peoples."

"I am absolutely certain," I agreed, "that you ought to have your independence. I think it would be good for you and good for all of us. Certainly the British have not shown any startling ability to defend their empire or to win its sympathy."

"You must say that to America," Gandhi urged.

"I will say it," I declared, "but not in those terms. We are now financing all of Britain's purchases of munitions. We are making sixty thousand planes this year, but a hundred and forty thousand in 1943. As far as America's role in India is concerned, the crisis here has matured a bit too early. [They laughed.] If we were making one hundred and forty thousand planes per year now and had two million men at the front, our views on India would receive more attention in London. The British do not understand today what is happening in Asia. With American help they may understand tomorrow."

"Therefore it is," Gandhi said, "that I come to brass tacks and say that the British will understand not while we are reasoning with them and showing them the great justice and feasibility of our proposal, but when we begin to act. That is British history. They are impressed by action, and it is action that we must take now. For the moment, however, I must popularize the idea of an Indian national government now and demonstrate that there is nothing chimerical or visionary about it. It is based on non-violence although I do not need the idea of non-violence to prove the validity or justice of my aim. The same aim might have evolved even if I were violently inclined. Even if I were violently inclined I might have said, 'Go and do not use India as your military base.' But today I say, 'If you must use India as a base lest someone else appropriate it, use it, and stay here on honorable terms and do no harm.' I would go further and add that if the central government which India evolves is military-minded the British may have its help.' "

"If the British," I asked, "under pressure, were to accept your offer, how would you launch your republic of seven hundred thousand villages?"

"I cannot give you a concrete plan," Gandhi said. "I cannot work it out today. It is all theoretical. It has to come out as a plan drafted by a body of representatives and not out of the brain of one whom many label a dreamer."

"Well," I said, "I am not so completely cast-iron as not to understand homespun cotton."

"But you do not understand vegetables," Gandhi said.

"I do not like the same vegetables every day for lunch and dinner." He laughed and we all laughed and I got up and left.

For three hours this afternoon Nehru and I sat in the one room of the guest house, he squatting on the bed, I on our single chair, and discussed human happiness, culture, how society could be improved so that men might lead honest lives, America, Russia, India, and so on. He is not as pro-Soviet as he used to be. But he is very pro-Chinese and has been talking to Gandhi today about China. There will be a give and take between them, and Gandhi will win Nehru over to the idea of a civil disobedience movement. Nehru had doubts when he came here. He was waiting for President Roosevelt to intervene again in the Indian situation and induce the British to compromise. But with the British adamantly refusing to negotiate for a wartime settlement of urgent Indian problems, Gandhi's logic of compulsion through non-violence be-

comes irresistible to an Indian nationalist like
Nehru.

I urged Nehru to go to America and talk with
President Roosevelt. I told him that Americans
spontaneously react in favor of any nation's desire
for independence and that, furthermore, America's economic interests in India were different
from those of Britain.

We also discussed the Hindu religion. Nehru
said that Hinduism has no fundamentalism and
that no Hindu therefore can be punished or ex-
communicated for being unorthodox. "You can
even be a Hindu and an atheist," he said. "As
Gandhi said this morning, 'You don't cease being
a Hindu because you do not believe in caste or in
untouchability.' In like manner, you can be a religious Hindu even if you hang Christ's picture on
your wall and believe in his precepts."

June 8, 1942

Nᴇʜʀᴜ sʟᴇᴘᴛ on a bed three feet from mine. He said that noises had disturbed him during the night. I never hear any noises. He told me he had come back last night at 9:15 from chatting with some friends in the ashram and thought he would spend the evening talking to me. But he found me sound asleep.

At six this morning Gandhi, surrounded by the usual group of eight or ten in white, went out for his usual walk. It is his silent day. He saw me on the porch and raised his arm high above his head in greeting. I spent the morning typing and talking to Nehru.

In the afternoon, Aryanaikam came over. He has studied with Dewey and Thorndike at Columbia University and took degrees at Edinburgh, Cambridge, and Oxford. He brought me a clean suit of white homespun khadi and also sandals, for he had noticed that the sand and gravel of Sevagram were wearing holes in my bedroom slip-

pers. Apropos of his studies in America, he recalled
a trip to New York on the "S.S. Berengaria" when
the dining-room steward refused to serve him because he was brown. That stuck in his soul. His
specialty is basic education, which means teaching
peasant children crafts, chiefly spinning and weav-
ing and agriculture. He said the Congress ministries had fostered this plan when they were in office
in the Provinces between 1937 and 1939. But the
British discouraged it. He showed me quotations
from official British reports on education in India
which stated that British methods had failed. He
contended that the sole purpose of the educational
system in India was to train clerks and government
officials to work for the British. The government
therefore was not interested, he said, in the education of the lower classes. It merely wished to edu-
cate part of the middle class which might serve it.
The result was middle-class nationalism. Recently
the British government had taken over the build-
ings of some teachers' training schools.

    Nehru, who had listened and agreed with Ar-
yanaikam, asserted that if the British had applied
to education a small part of what they spent on
arms in peace-time in India the Indian peasant
would not be so illiterate. Aryanaikam said the
British always pleaded lack of funds to establish an
adequate number of schools. He showed me the

official British census figures: in 1921, seven per cent of the population of India were literate; in 1931, this had gone up to eight per cent. "Just imagine," Aryanaikam exclaimed with an irony that was obviously painful to him, "one per cent increase in ten years." The 1941 figures on illiteracy have been pronounced unreliable.

Gandhi's silence ended early enough to enable him to receive me at three this afternoon for my usual daily interview. I started by saying that we had not even mentioned India's biggest problem, the problem most difficult of solution.

"What's that?" Gandhi demanded.

"India's population," I stated, "is increasing by five million each year. British official statistics show that the population of India increased from three hundred and thirty-eight million in 1931 to three hundred and eighty-eight million in 1941. Fifty million more mouths to feed and bodies to clothe and shelter. Fifty million more in ten years. How are you going to deal with that?"

"One of the answers might be birth control," Gandhi said. "But I am opposed to birth control."

"I am not," I said, "but in a backward country like India birth control could not be very effective anyway."

"Then perhaps we need some good epidemics," Gandhi laughed.

"Or a good civil war," I suggested gloomily. "But," I went on, "Soviet Russia had famines, epidemics, and a civil war and yet her population grew very rapidly, and the Bolsheviks, in 1928, took certain economic measures."

"You want to force me into an admission that we would need rapid industrialization," Gandhi said. "I will not be forced into such an admission. Our first problem is to get rid of British rule. Then we will be free, without restraints from the outside, to do what India requires. The British have seen fit to allow us to have some factories and also to prohibit other factories. No! For me the paramount problem is the ending of British domination."

This, obviously, was what he wanted to talk about; the vague future interested him less. "Well," I asked, "how do you actually see your impending civil disobedience movement? What shape will it take?"

"In the villages," Gandhi explained, "the peasants will stop paying taxes. They will make salt despite official prohibition. This seems a small matter; the salt tax yields only a paltry sum to the British government. But refusal to pay it will give the peasants the courage to think that they are capable of independent action. Their next step will be to seize the land."

"With violence?" I asked.

"There may be violence, but then again the landlords may cooperate."

"You are an optimist," I said.

"They might cooperate by fleeing," Gandhi said.

Nehru, who had been sitting by my side, said, "They might vote for confiscation with their legs just as you say in your *Men and Politics* that, as Lenin put it, the Russian soldier voted for peace with his legs in 1917—he ran away from the trenches. So also the Indian landowners might vote for the confiscation of their land by running away from the village."

"Or," I said, "they might organize violent resistance."

"There may be fifteen days of chaos," Gandhi speculated, "but I think we could soon bring that under control."

"You feel then that it must be confiscation without compensation?" I asked.

"Of course," Gandhi agreed. "It would be financially impossible for anybody to compensate the landlords."

"That accounts for the villages," I said. "But that is not all of India."

"No," Gandhi stated. "Workingmen in the cities would leave their factories. The railroads would stop running."

"General strike," I said to myself. "I know," I

said aloud, "that you have in the past had a large following among the peasants, but your city working-class support is not so big."

"No," Gandhi acquiesced, "not so big. But this time the workingmen will act too, because, as I sense the mood of the country, everybody wants freedom, Hindus, Moslems, Untouchables, Sikhs, workers, peasants, industrialists, Indian civil servants, and even the Princes. The Princes know that a new wind is blowing. Things cannot go on as they have been. We cannot support a war which may perpetuate British domination. How can we fight for democracy in Japan, Germany, and Italy when India is not democratic? I want to save China. I want no harm to come to China. But to collaborate we must be free. Slaves do not fight for freedom."

"Do you think," I asked, "that the Moslems will follow you in your civil disobedience movement?"

"Not perhaps in the beginning," Gandhi said. "But they will come in when they see that the movement is succeeding."

"Might not the Moslems be used to interfere with or stop the movement?"

"Undoubtedly," Gandhi agreed, "their leaders might try or the government might try, but the Moslem millions do not oppose independence and they could not, therefore, oppose our measures to bring about that independence. The Moslem masses sympathize with the one over-all goal of Congress: freedom for India. That is the solid rock on which Hindu-Moslem unity can be built."

I made one last effort to bring the conversation back to the question of excess population. I could only get him to say that, "If there is large-scale industrialization, the state will of course have to lead the process."

In the evening I went over to Mahadev Desai's hut and watched him spin. He is the editor of *Harijan,* Gandhi's English-language weekly, and he helped Gandhi to write his autobiography. He said he gave up his law practice at the age of twenty-five and has been closely associated with Gandhi ever since; that is, for the last twenty-five years. He told me that my talks with Gandhi have been the most important that he has had with any foreigner since 1939. He keeps complete notes of everything that Gandhi says, and he has notes of my conversations too. As we sat on the floor, I could understand how relaxing and pacifying the motions of spinning could be.

"All these days," I said to Desai, "I have been listening carefully to Gandhi, and recording his words after each interview, and then rereading them and thinking about them and trying to fathom the source of Gandhi's great influence. I have come to the conclusion, tentatively, that the chief reason for that influence is Gandhi's passion."

"That is right," Desai said.

"What is the root of his passion?" I asked.

"This passion," Desai explained, "is the sublimation of all the passions that flesh is heir to."

"Sex?"

"Sex and anger and personal ambition. Gandhi can admit that he is wrong. He can chastise himself and take the blame for the mistakes of others, as when he called off a civil disobedience movement because it became violent. Gandhi is under his own complete control. That generates tremendous energy and passion within him."

I have an impression that these Indians are much more honest than Westerners. They talk more honestly about themselves. They are more self-analytical and self-critical.

I HAVE DECIDED to leave tomorrow for Hyderabad, the capital of the native state of Hyderabad
where the Nizam, richest man in the world, rules
some sixteen million people with British help. I
could stay here for several more days, and Gandhi
yesterday asked me to stay on, but I had come to
Sevagram with the intention of remaining only
two or three days and now I must be on my way.
By five-thirty A.M. I had shaved and breakfasted
and went over to where Gandhi was having his
mango meal. "At one time," he said, "in Bengal,
when I was working very hard, I lived entirely on
mangoes."

"An Englishman or an American, if he were
working very hard," I said, "would have lived entirely on beefsteak."

"That's the difference," Gandhi said. "The British have no variety in their vegetables either. It is
always potatoes and cabbage."

While we talked Kano Gandhi, the Mahatma's
nephew, took photographs of us.

When we started on our walk, I said, "I have found you so objective about your work and the world that I want to ask you to be objective about yourself. This isn't a personal question but a political question: how do you account for your influence over so many people?"

"I can see the spirit in which you ask this," Gandhi said. "I think my influence is due to the fact that I pursue the truth. That is my goal."

"I do not underestimate the power of truth," I argued. "But this explanation seems to me inadequate. Leaders like Hitler have achieved power by telling lies. That doesn't mean that you cannot become influential by telling the truth. But truth in itself has not always availed others in this country or elsewhere. Why is it," I continued, "that you, without any of the paraphernalia of power, without a government or police behind you, without ceremonies or even a tightly knit organization, for I understand that Congress is in no sense a disciplined, tightly coordinated body, how is it that you have been able to sway so many millions and get them to sacrifice their comforts and time and even their lives?"

"Truth," he said, "is not merely a matter of words. It is really a matter of living the truth." He stopped, and I felt he meant me to think of the simple life which he led. "It is true, I have not much equipment. My education is not great. I do not read much." He paused.

"Isn't it," I suggested, "that when you advocate independence you strike a chord in many Indians? A musician does something to the members of his audience. You play a note which Indians are waiting to hear. I have noticed that people applaud most the arias they have heard often and liked. A lecture audience applauds views it agrees with. Is it that you say and do what your people want you to say and do?"

"Yes," he said, "maybe that is it. I was a loyalist in respect to the British, and then I became a rebel. I was a loyalist until 1896."

"Weren't you also a loyalist between 1914 and 1918?"

"Yes, in a way," he affirmed, "but not really. By 1918 I had already said that British rule in India is an alien rule and must end." He remained silent as we trudged along. Finally he said, "I will tell you how it happened that I decided to urge the departure of the British. It was in 1916. I was in Lucknow working for Congress. A peasant came up to me looking like any other peasant of India, poor and emaciated. He said, 'My name is Rajkumar Shukla. I am from Champaran, and I want you to come to my district.' He described the misery of his fellow agriculturists and prayed me to let him take me to Champaran, which was hundreds of miles from Lucknow. He begged so insistently and persuasively that I promised. But he wanted me to fix the date. I could not do that. For

weeks and weeks Rajkumar Shukla followed me
wherever I went over the face of India. He stayed
wherever I stayed. At length, early in 1917, I had
to be in Calcutta. Rajkumar followed me and ultimately persuaded me to take the train with him
from Calcutta to Champaran. Champaran is a district where indigo is planted. I decided that I
would talk to thousands of peasants but, in order
to get the other side of the question, I would also
interview the British commissioner of the area.
When I called on the commissioner he bullied me
and advised me to leave immediately. I did not accept his advice and proceeded on the back of an
elephant to one of the villages. A police messenger
overtook us and served notice on me to leave
Champaran. I allowed the police to escort me back
to the house where I was staying and then I decided to offer civil resistance. I would not leave
the district. Huge crowds gathered around the
house. I cooperated with the police in regulating
the crowds. A kind of friendly relationship sprang
up between me and the police. That day in Champaran became a red-letter day in my life. I was put
on trial. The government attorney pleaded with
the magistrate to postpone the case but I asked him
to go on with it. I wanted to announce publicly
that I had disobeyed the order to leave Champaran. I told him that I had come to collect informa-
tion about local conditions and that I therefore

had to disobey the British law because I was acting in obedience with a higher law, with the voice of my conscience. This was my first act of civil disobedience against the British. My desire was to establish the principle that no Englishman had the right to tell me to leave any part of my country where I had gone for a peaceful pursuit. The government begged me repeatedly to drop my plea of guilty. Finally the magistrate closed the case. Civil disobedience had won. It became the method by which India could be made free."

"This," I said, "is perhaps another clue to your position in India."

"What I did," he interrupted, "was a very ordinary thing. I declared that the British could not order me around in my own country."

"It was ordinary," I commented, "but you were the first to do it. It's like the story of Columbus and the egg."

"What's that?" he asked.

"Have you never heard the story of Columbus and the egg?" I asked Gandhi.

"No," he confessed, "tell me."

I told him. He laughed. "That's right," he said, "it was an ordinary thing to say that I had the right to go peacefully anywhere in my own country. But no one had said it before."

By this time we had returned to Gandhi's house.

At three o'clock I came for my regular interview. Gandhi, who had been talking to Nehru for an hour, asked me to excuse him for ten minutes. He had to go to the lavatory, he explained. When he came back he lay down on his pallet, and one of his secretaries handed him a letter that had come in the mail. Gandhi took it and smiled as he read it, then turned two pages and I saw a folded sheet of music. Turning to Kurshed who was in the room, he said laughingly to her, "Here, sing this for me." She hummed the notes and read some of the verses, and then I asked for the letter and the music. She gave them to me and I brought them to America with me. The letter was dated "United States of America, Hollywood, California, 1535 North Hobart Boulevard, March 10, 1942." It was addressed to "Mahatma Gandhi, Indian National Congress, India," and signed by Marius Mannik. The letter read, "My Dear Mahatma Gandhi: Am sending you this song in a democratic spirit and hope you will receive it as such. I have long been one of your admirers. Most sincerely yours." The song was entitled "Let's Beat the Axis" and was dedicated to "General Douglas MacArthur and his forces." The chorus read:

"So let us grind our Axes to beat the cruel Axis,
   Our Faith and Work and Taxes must stay the foe that whacks us;
   Then let us grind our Axes and beat the cruel Axis
   Till tyranny relaxes from Nome to old Damascus."

When the laughing subsided, Gandhi turned to me and said, "Now fire."

"That would be violence, Mr. Gandhi," I said.

"And have you any objection to violence?" he asked.

"But you have never heard a word from me as to whether I am for or against violence," I said.

"You don't have to tell me," he said laughingly. "I look at you and know."

"In case your impending civil disobedience movement," I asked, "develops a violent phase, as it has sometimes in past years, would you call it off? You have done that before."

"In my present mood," he replied, "it would be incorrect to say that no circumstances might arise in which I would call off the movement. In the past, however, I have been too cautious. That was necessary for my own training and for the training of my collaborators. But I would not behave as I have in the past."

"Since I am going away soon from your village," I began, "I want to be quite sure that I understand your ideas correctly. Would there be any chance of a compromise between what you want and what the British authorities are ready to offer? Might some kind of a modified Cripps proposal be acceptable to you?"

"No," Gandhi said. "Nothing along the lines of the Cripps offer. I want their complete and irrevocable withdrawal. I am essentially a man of compromise because I am never sure that I am right. But now it is the unbending future in me that is uppermost. There is no halfway house between withdrawal and non-withdrawal. It is, of course, no complete physical withdrawal that I ask. I shall insist, however, on the transfer of political power from the British to the Indian people."

"What about the time factor?" I inquired. "When you launch your civil disobedience movement, and if the British yield, will it be a matter of the immediate transfer of political power?"

"The British," he said, "would not have to do that in two days or in two weeks. But it must be irrevocable and complete political withdrawal."

"Suppose the British say they will withdraw completely after the war?" I asked.

"No," he said. "In that case my proposal loses much of its value. I want them to go now so I can help China and Russia. Today I am unable to pull my full weight in favor of them. It is my philanthropy that has made me present this proposal. For the time being, India disappears from my gaze. I never wanted independence for India's sake alone. I never wished to play the role of frog-in-the-well."

"You have not felt this way before, Mr. Gandhi," I suggested.

"The whole idea," he explained, "keeps blossoming out within me. The original idea of asking the British to go burst upon me suddenly. It was the Cripps fiasco that inspired the idea. Hardly had he gone when it seized hold of me."

"Exactly when did the idea occur to you?" I asked.

"Soon after Cripps's departure. I wrote a letter to Horace Alexander [a British friend of India] in reply to his letter to me. Thereafter the idea possessed me. Then began the propaganda. Later I framed a resolution. My first feeling was, We need an answer to Cripps's failure. What a diabolical thing if the Cripps mission were without any redeeming feature. Suppose I ask them to go. This idea arose from the crushed hope that had been pretty high in our minds. We had heard good things about Cripps from Jawaharlal and others. Yet the whole mission fell flat. How, I asked myself, am I to remedy this situation? The presence of the British blocks our way. It was during my Monday day of silence that the idea was born in me. From that silence arose so many thoughts that the silence possessed me and the thoughts possessed me too and I knew I had to act for Russia and China and India. My heart goes out to China. I cannot forget my five hours with Chiang Kai-shek and his attractive partner. Even for China's sake alone I must do this. I am burdening my thoughts with the world's sorrow."

"Why will it not wait until after the war?" I asked.

"Because I want to act now and be useful while the war is here," he replied.

"Have you any organization with which to carry on this struggle?" I inquired.

"The organization is the Congress Party," he answered. "But if it fails me, I have my own organization, myself. I am a man possessed by an idea. If such a man cannot get an organization, he becomes an organization."

"Have you sufficient confidence in the present mood of the country? Will it follow you? This civil disobedience movement may involve heavy sacrifices for the people. Has anybody opposed your idea?"

"I had a letter today from Rajagopalachari," he told me. "He is the only one opposed. I know his views. But how does he expect the Moslem League to work with him when he wishes to work with the Moslem League in order to destroy Pakistan?"

"Do you think Jinnah is set on Pakistan? Perhaps it is a bargaining counter with him which he will give up if Hindu-Moslem cooperation can be achieved."

"As I have told you before," Gandhi stated, "he will only give it up when the British are gone and when there is therefore nobody with whom to bargain."

"So you intend to tell the British in advance when you will launch your movement?" I said.

"Yes," he confirmed.

"You had better not tell them too far in advance," I laughed.

"Is that a tip from you?" he laughed.

"No," I said.

"They will know in good time," he assured me.

"If you look at this in its historic perspective," I said, you are doing a novel and remarkable thing —you are ordaining the end of an empire."

"Even a child can do that," he said. "I will appeal to the people's instincts. I may arouse them."

"Let us try," I suggested, "to see the possible reaction throughout the world. Your very friends, China and Russia, may appeal to you not to launch this civil disobedience movement."

"Let them appeal to me. I may be dissuaded. But if I can get appeals to them in time, I may convert them. If you have access to men in authority here, tell them this. You are a fine listener. No humbug about you. Discuss this with them and let them show me if there are any flaws in my proposal."

"Have I your authority," I asked, "to say this to the Viceroy?"

"Yes, you have my permission," he said firmly. "Let him talk to me; I may be converted. I am a reasonable man. I would not like to take any step that would harm China."

"Or America?" I suggested.

"If America were hurt, it would hurt everybody," he said.

"Would you wish President Roosevelt to be informed about your attitude?"

"Yes," he said. "I do not wish to appeal to anybody. But I would want Mr. Roosevelt to know my plans, my views, and my readiness to compromise. Tell your President I wish to be dissuaded."

"Do you expect drastic action when you launch the movement?" I asked.

"Yes," he answered. "I expect it any day. I am ready. I know I may be arrested. I am ready."

Mahadev Desai, Gandhi's secretary, came to see me this afternoon and brought me a copy of Gandhi's autobiography. He said Gandhi had talked to him about what I might do after my departure, and he and Gandhi had agreed that I could convey to Roosevelt and to the Viceroy any part of my conversations with Gandhi. Desai declared that Gandhi wished to discuss the situation with the Viceroy.

At dinner today Gandhi said two things would happen when I was gone: "Kurshed Ben will miss you because she will have nobody to take care of, and I will miss you during the hour which has been reserved for you every afternoon." I told Gandhi that I should have liked to stay for a long time and maybe I would return when the Congress Working Committee assembled at Wardha to act upon his decision to launch the civil disobedience campaign. "It will meet within a fortnight," Gandhi informed me. "But come back whenever you like." Then he asked me whether I had slept well in Sevagram. I replied that I had slept better than I had for many years.

"It is good to sleep under the stars," he said. "The best thing. But I suppose," he added, "that would be impossible in Russia." I told him it was very hot in some parts of Russia.

"Oh," he exclaimed, "I thought it was always cold in Russia."

I sat in the guest house with Kurshed and Nehru. Both had been in Indian prisons many times. I got them to talk about life in prison. They said that important leaders received good accommodations and that Gandhi was always well treated and was able to obtain the food he wished. Also Gandhi's correspondence with people outside jail was not interfered with. Others, however, could not communicate freely with free people. Members of Congress who were in prison never tried to escape, Nehru explained, because Congress members deliberately courted arrest by openly practicing civil disobedience. There was nothing underground or secret in any one of Gandhi's campaigns of resistance to the British raj. Congress first proclaimed its intention to resist and then resisted, and if a Congress prisoner were to escape, it would only be to commit a further immediate act of civil disobedience and be put back in jail again.

Nehru was now in complete agreement with Gandhi about the coming campaign. He had hesitated to follow Gandhi because he had hoped that President Roosevelt or Chiang Kai-shek or somebody else would intervene in the Indian situation, break the Anglo-Indian deadlock, and make organized opposition to the British unnecessary. Nehru had been anti-Axis long before many high officials in democratic countries. He had opposed the appeasement policies of democratic governments and was on record as being actively anti-Japanese, anti-Mussolini, and anti-Hitler. He did not wish to embarrass the British in their war against the Axis. But he felt that the British had to be forced to take the steps which would save them from reverses in India similar to those they had suffered in the Far East. He did not feel that the British could successfully defend India with the military strength available to them. They should therefore have the wisdom, he said, to adopt measures which would enlist the support of the Indian people in the defense of their country.

THIS IS my last day at Sevagram. I was up at five. Nehru had already left his bed and gone over to talk to Gandhi. He returned at seven and said that he and President Azad of the Congress Party were going to Wardha today and that Gandhi would follow soon for some private discussions with them. We arranged that I would go with them to Wardha and there take the train for Hyderabad. Members of the ashram started appearing to say goodbye to me. They were all very sweet, and I felt they had been extremely good to me. Mahadev Desai came, took me aside, and talked with me about the possibility of Gandhi's arrest. He said he had heard rumors that Gandhi would be arrested on June 17. I said I doubted it and expressed the view that the British would wait until Congress definitely adopted a resolution to start civil disobedience. Desai said it was a pity that I was not going immediately to New Delhi, since Gandhi wanted to see the Viceroy and hoped that I could arrange the interview. Gandhi believed that if he could talk to the Viceroy they would arrive at an understanding, Desai said.

At about noon—the temperature must have been 110—Azad, Nehru, and I got into the car and travelled over the hot dusty road to the Congress hostel in Wardha. It was a five-mile trip. Azad is a big man with a tough body, big head, short gray goatee, gray short-cropped hair, a strong voice. His skin is lighter than that of most Indians. His family came to India from Arabia four hundred years ago. He is one of the best-known Moslems of India. He has translated the Koran into Urdu and is a recognized authority on Arabic lore and on the history of Islam. Everybody addresses him as "the Maulana," which means Moslem scholar and divine.

The three of us lunched in a cool room at the hostel. For the first time in eight days I enjoyed the refreshing effect of an electric fan. After lunch I interviewed Azad. Nehru interpreted. Azad understands English but hesitates to speak it, and so Nehru did not translate my questions and only translated Azad's remarks. Azad, who had conducted most of the negotiations with Cripps, said that Cripps had been a disappointment to him. He had expected Cripps to be a friend of India. Cripps had told him definitely that there would be a new Indian national government which would function as a responsible cabinet with the Viceroy interfering as little in policy-making as the King in England. It was on this assumption that the negotiations with Sir Stafford proceeded. They had practically agreed on a formula for dividing the defense of India between the British Commander-in-Chief and the Indian Defense Minister. Then quite suddenly, on April 9, Azad stated, Cripps told him that the British government refused to terminate the Viceroy's veto power. Thereupon, the negotiations with Cripps broke down. Azad felt that Cripps had made a promise and then discovered that London would not let him keep it. The key to an agreement between Britain and India, Azad declared, is the formation of an Indian provisional coalition cabinet government. The Congress Party did not expect to have a majority of the members of this cabinet, Azad declared.

I asked him what was the mood of the Indian people after the failure of Cripps. He replied, "In part it is one of helplessness. There is also an element of protest. But chiefly it is the feeling that there was no use trying to reach an understanding with the British government. The British have decided to give up nothing. Many Moslems have this impression too."

Azad said that in the present political climate of India, no Moslem leader could oppose independence. The Moslem League, he declared, was reactionary and depended chiefly on the support of landlords. Ninety-five per cent of the Moslems of India were descended from Hindus. The rest came in with the Moslem conquerors. But even those— his family included—had become assimilated. In Bengal, he said, repeating what Gandhi had told me, the Hindus and Moslems speak Bengali and dress and live alike. In Madras, they all spoke Tamil. In the villages, the differences between the religious communities were small. Jinnah did not want Pakistan, Azad declared, except as a bargaining card against the Hindus, and England had obligingly given it to him.

Both Nehru and Azad assured me that nobody in India wanted the Moslems to remain in an Indian union if they really wished to secede. "However," Azad said, "I do not believe in divorce before marriage. If the Hindus and Moslems try to live together and fail, then there can be a separation. But a large number of Moslems believe in the unity of India and they do not wish to disrupt that unity before it is given a fair trial."

At three o'clock in the afternoon Gandhi burst into the hostel. I was near the entrance when he arrived. His face was wreathed in smiles. The car which had brought Nehru, Azad, and me to Wardha had returned to Sevagram to fetch Gandhi and Desai. When it was three-quarters of a mile from Wardha, the car broke down. Gandhi got out and walked that distance under the broiling Indian afternoon sun. When he reached the hostel he was triumphant, and commented on the unreliability of these "new-fangled technical achievements of the industrial age."

Within a few minutes, Gandhi was closeted with Azad and Nehru. I walked into the room through the open door, but they were talking Hindustani, and so I left. Later Grover, the young Associated Press correspondent in India, arrived for an interview. Gandhi said to him that India now was a corpse and as a corpse it could not help much in winning the war. He wanted India to be free from British political domination and then India would rise in her strength to defend herself.

I left Wardha at nine-thirty P.M. Gandhi shook me firmly by the hand as I said goodbye and asked me to visit him again.

I flew back from India to New York in seven days. Shortly after my return, a reporter interviewed me and asked if I had written Gandhi a bread-and-butter letter. It had not occurred to me to do so.

Aᴆᴛᴇʀ I had left his village, Gandhi sent me a letter for President Roosevelt. In a handwritten note accompanying this letter, Gandhi wrote: "If it does not commend itself to you, you may tear it to pieces. If it is something else you want, you may tell me." Gandhi has little vanity.

Gandhi never hesitates to admit error, and by preference he does so publicly. In May, 1942, as a consequence of the failure of Sir Stafford Cripps's mission, Gandhi announced that "The British Must Go." They must withdraw their troops, he said, or else he would start a campaign of civil disobedience. In June, however, he altered this demand. "There was obviously a gap in my first writing," he confessed in an article *Harijan,* his weekly magazine. "I filled it in as soon as it was discovered by one of my numerous interviewers. Non-violence demands the strictest honesty, cost what it may. The public have therefore to suffer my weakness, if weakness it be. I could not be guilty of ask-

114

ing the Allies to take a step which would involve certain defeat. . . . Abrupt withdrawals of the Allied troops might result in Japan's occupation of India and China's sure fall. I had not the remotest idea of any such catastrophe resulting from my action. Therefore, I feel that if, in spite of the acceptance of my proposal [to liberate India] it is deemed necessary by the Allies to remain in India to prevent Japanese occupation, they should do so. . . ."

The ordinary politician, when he seeks office or the adoption of his policy, will promise you peace and prosperity, lower taxes, higher profits—in fact, the moon and the stars, if you support him. Gandhi's life goal is freedom for his country. He ought, therefore, to assure England and the world that if this end-all of his career is granted everything will be well in India. Instead he says: "I am not sure that there will be order after the British leave. There could be chaos. I have said: 'Let the British go in an orderly fashion and leave India to God! You may not like such unrealistic language. Then call it anarchy. That is the worst that can happen. But there may not be anarchy. We will try to prevent it." Such a statement, however, enables Gandhi's critics to say, "Gandhi predicts chaos if the British leave."

Gandhi asserts that when the British transfer power to Indians the Indian army is to be disbanded. But a moment earlier he has said: "Naturally there will be no prohibition against any Indian giving his own personal help by way of being a recruit or/and of giving financial aid." And at another time, (in *Harijan,* August 6, 1942) he wrote: "Cannot a limitless number of soldiers be trained out of India's millions? Would they not make as good fighting material as any in the world?" What does it all mean? Is Gandhi simply contradicting himself? No. He wants to disband the Indian army which consists of men who have "volunteered" because they were hungry and expected to eat well as soldiers or who were impressed into the services. But then India can recruit its own national army. This shows, however, with what ease Gandhi can be mischievously misquoted out of context.

Part of the pleasure of intimate intellectual contact with Gandhi is that he really opens his mind and allows the interviewer to see how the machine inside works. When most people talk they try to bring their ideas out in final perfect form so that they are least exposed to attack. Not so with Gandhi. He gives immediate expression to each step in his thinking. It is as though a writer were to publish the first draft of his story, and then the second draft, and ultimately third and last draft. Readers might protest, and claim that the plot had been changed, that the popular lover had been transformed into a villain, and so forth. Gandhi would not listen to such protests. He would say, Yes, I changed my mind. Actually, he thinks aloud, and the entire process is for the record. This confuses some people and impels others to say he contradicts himself, or that he is a hypocrite. Gandhi does not care. Maybe he is too old and impersonal and not of this world to bother about the impression he makes. Many Indians and Englishmen in India, when I interviewed them, cautioned me that their words were not for publication. Gandhi never worried about what I would write about him or how I would quote him. He did not talk at me; he talked to me. I spent many hours with Mohammed Ali Jinnah, the President of the Moslem League of India. He is a brilliant parliamentarian, a skilled debater, and an incorruptible politician. But he talked at me. He was trying to convince me. When I put a question to him I felt as though it had turned on a phonograph record. I had heard it all before or could have read it in the literature he gave me. But when I asked Gandhi something I felt that I had started a creative process. I could see and hear his mind work. With Jinnah I could only hear the needle scratch the phonograph record. Jinnah gave me nothing but his conclusions. But I could follow Gandhi as he moved to a conclusion. He is, therefore, much more exciting than Jinnah. If you strike right with Gandhi you open a new pocket of thought. An interview with him is a voyage of discovery, and he himself is sometime surprised at the things he says. His secretaries, who sat with us as he spoke, were often surprised at the novelty of his assertions. That is why I learned so much from Gandhi and so much about Gandhi. He did not merely give me fact and opinions. He revealed himself. He also supplied one with ammunition against himself. Gandhi did not have to tell me, for instance, that he had ascribed qualities to his weekly day of silence which he knew it did not possess. But that is Gandhi. His brain has no blue pencil; he doesn't censor himself. This makes him a baffling or even irritating person to some politicians. He says, for instance, that if he had the opportunity, he would go to Japan and try to end the war. He knows, and immediately adds, that he would never get the opportunity to go, and if he went, Japan would not make peace. Then why did he say he would go to Japan? Because he thought it. As a pacifist he would really like to bring about a cessation of hostilities. The fact that this hope is impracticable is for Gandhi not reason not to mention it.

Gandhi sometimes takes delight in expounding ideas which are impractical anachronisms. He scoffs at modern inventions. He is aware that he cannot turn back the clock. He cannot abolish the automobile. But he can make fun of it. He asserts that a federal administration is not necessarily. If you point out the difficulties that would arise in the absence of a federal administration, he is unconvinced. Then you argue further and he finally says, "I know that despite my personal views there will be a central administration." This is a characteristic Gandhi cycle: He enunciates a principle, defends it, and ultimately admits that it is unworkable. His mind is malleable and fluid. There is something of the dictator in him when he wants action. Then he crushes opposition by the weight of his logic and the strength of his popular following. But there is nothing of the dictator in his thinking. A dictator can never admit he is wrong. Gandhi can; he often does.

Gandhi is very much of a Hindu. The Hindu religion is a tolerant and sponge-like religion. Hindus believe in one God. Some also believe in Christ. Some are atheists; they claim that Hinduism is a code of life independent of a deity. Some pray to idols. Some worship mountains and rivers and gods who were once men and women; they see no conflict between such opposites as monotheism and idolatry. "If the Niagara Falls were in India," an Indian said to me, "they would be a god." The Mt. Olympus of Hinduism is densely populated, but many Hindus are sure that there is a place reserved in it for Mahatma Gandhi.

The general Indian feeling about Gandhi is that

he has devoted his life to the people. He lives like the people and shares their primitive hardships and poverty. He has no money and no property. He wants only one thing—a free India. And since so many millions of Indians want the same thing, Gandhi has become the symbol of a nation's yearning.

Everywhere in India, whenever an Indian criticized the British I would insist that he explain to me why he was anti-British. I said to an Indian Moslem who is a high civil servant in the British government, "Why are so many Indians anti-British?"

"Why shouldn't we be?" he exclaimed. "That is the more appropriate question." No nation likes the foreign nation which rules it, he added.

Gandhi has devoted Moslem followers and Hindu followers, and Parsis and Untouchables who believe in him because he, more than any other man, has striven for decades to free his country. Many of them differ with Gandhi on numerous questions. There are Moslems who accuse him of wanting to establish Hindu rule. But few deny the constancy of his labors for national redemption. In modern times, the urge towards nationhood has been elemental, natural, and instinctive. Gandhi is the most forceful Indian exponent of this urge.

Gandhi has the conviction that he can, sitting in

his hut at Sevagram, reading his correspondence, and listening to the Indians who visit him, sense the sentiment and hear the prayers of the Indian masses. He is persuaded that he knows what they want and is, therefore, entitled to act for them. Gandhi is immersed in India. He identifies himself with India. All his antennae are out to catch the voice of India. He hears it. He is sure he interprets it correctly. Such a certainty is often the motive power and guiding light of leaders. Gandhi may have doubts about his views on economics and sociology. He will consent to modify methods and the time-table. But he is undeviating, unyielding and uncompromising on the central issue of independence. Indians tell you Gandhi was born to achieve independence. He is ready to die for it. Sacrifice and renunciation rank very high in the Indian calendar of virtues.

Gandhi's wisdom, his shrewdness, and his profound religiousness in a nation that is the most religious nation in the world further explain his preeminence. But his strongest popular appeal is his desire for national freedom and the impatient passion with which he drives towards that goal. I think the yearning for India's independence takes precedence in him over everything else, even over his belief in non-violence. At least, he can work on terms of the friendliest cooperation with men like Nehru, Azad, and Rajagopalachari who, he knows, are not pacifists, but he could not work with enemies of Indian freedom.

In his pursuit of independence there is a musical harmony between Gandhi and millions of Indians. Great leaders must have this harmony; it is the source of their greatness. Winston Churchill has manifested it in many of his speeches. He says brilliantly what so many plain English citizens say crudely to their neighbors or say to themselves at night. You follow a leader who is you in a better edition. Gandhi is father and brother to millions of semi-naked, half-starved, not-too-intellectual peasants and workingmen who want to attain dignity and prosperity through national effort. He is a chip of their block. He also answers the prayers of innumerable highly cultured Indians and mighty industrialists who resent the foreign yoke or even the mere presence of an outside overlord.

Gandhi's life is single-tracked; he wants a free India. That, too, is characteristic of great men. Churchill's one absorbing purpose is the preservation of Britain as a first-class power. Lenin's was the lifting of Russia out of the feudal mire. Lincoln's was union. Hitler's is world conquest. A big man is all of one piece like good sculpture.

A group of photographs taken during the author's stay in India. The pictures of Gandhi were taken by Kano Gandhi, a nephew; all other pictures were taken by a Bombay photographer, D. G. Tendulkar.

Gandhi's hut at Sevagram. Note the emblem of the Charkha, spinning wheel, beside the window.

Mahatma Gandhi and Louis Fischer in Sevagram, June, 194

scher prepares to ask Gandhi a question

Gandhi ponders the questio

oth enjoy a joke

Getting ready to go for a wa[lk]

Gandhi leans on the shoulders of two young followers during his daily walk.

Smiling at a Gandhi jok

arly morning interview

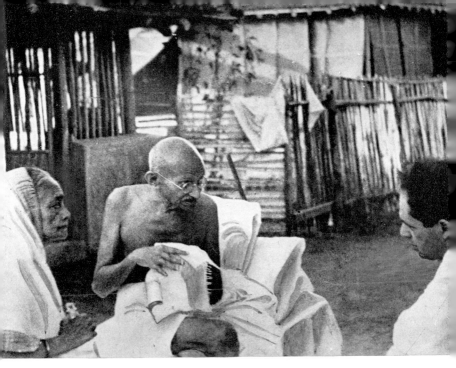

Gandhi has just finished breakfa

Nehru, Nehru's sister, Mrs. Krishna Hutheesing, and Fischer. The picture was taken in Mrs. Hutheesing's house in Bombay. It was in this house that Nehru was arrested recently.

Nehru and Fisch

Mohammed Ali Jinnah, president of the Moslem League of India,
and Fischer. The picture was taken at Jinnah's house in Malabar,
Bombay.

Jinnah and Fischer in the garden of Jinnah by the se

Dr. Ambedkar, in gray suit, leader of the Untouchables. The picture was taken in the slums of Bombay.